Global growth continues to slow, risking further divergence

- The growth of the world economy remains slow and uneven following the lingering impacts of the coronavirus disease (COVID-19) pandemic, the Russian invasion of Ukraine, and monetary policy tightening to combat high inflation. The International Monetary Fund downgraded global growth from 3.5% in 2022 to 3.0% in 2023 and 2.9% in 2024. Although the United States (US) economy has been more resilient thus far and is expected to grow by 2.1% in 2023 and 1.5% in 2024, growth in other advanced economies has been slower—particularly in the European Union where growth is projected at 0.7% in 2023 and 1.2% in 2024. Meanwhile, the economic performance of emerging markets and developing economies remains robust with growth expected to decline modestly to 4.0% in both 2023 and 2024 compared to 4.1% in 2022. Some risks—such as severe financial instability—have moderated, but the overall outlook remains tilted to the downside. Further worsening of the real estate crisis in the People's Republic of China (PRC)—which represents a complex policy challenge—could have consequences for the global economy. Renewed geopolitical tensions and climate-related disruptions could trigger more commodity price volatility, particularly for fuel and food prices. Inflation pressures remain despite a generally decelerating trend. Further monetary tightening could exacerbate already eroded fiscal buffers and elevated debt levels. Current conditions appear consistent with a "soft landing" scenario, but fiscal policy needs to be aligned with the "tighter-for-longer" stance of monetary policy.

- Developing Asia has benefited from healthy domestic demand, the reopening of the PRC, and rebounding tourism, although soft external demand has weighed on export-oriented economies. The regional growth forecast is 4.9% for 2023 and 4.8% for 2024. Although there is variation across economies, inflation pressures have generally subsided and the growth in consumer prices is forecast to decline to 3.5% in 2023 and 3.6% in 2024. This has allowed some central banks to ease monetary policy, which would support growth over the forecast horizon. Nonetheless, downside risks to the outlook have strengthened, particularly the persisting weakness of the PRC's property sector. Supply disruptions and an expected El Niño pose policy challenges for food security across the region. Continued vigilance is also needed to guard against financial stability risks from tighter global financial conditions.

- Recovery in tourism and spending on infrastructure have continued to drive Pacific economies, and the subregion is expected to grow by 3.5% in 2023 and 2.9% in 2024, largely driven by higher growth in Fiji. Subdued growth of 2.0% in 2023 is seen for Papua New Guinea—the subregion's largest economy—because of lower-than-expected growth in non-resource sectors along with foreign exchange shortages, but the forecast for 2024 remains unchanged at 2.6%. The Cook Islands, Fiji, Samoa, and Tonga have seen a strong recovery in tourism while other economies are benefiting from a resurgence in public construction, enabled by eased mobility restrictions and reduced logistics bottlenecks. These same growth drivers are expected to sustain economic expansion in 2024, but capacity constraints on the supply of labor and tourism facilities pose significant downside risks to growth. Vulnerability to disasters and climate events such as El Niño also continue to have potential implications for growth and inflation.

GDP Growth (%, annual)

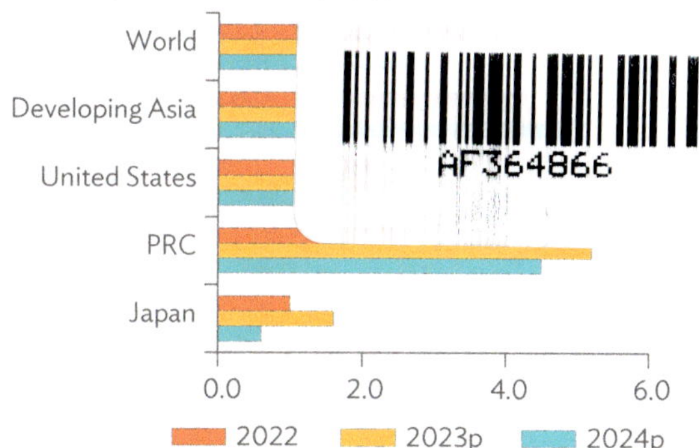

ADB = Asian Development Bank, p = projection, PRC = People's Republic of China.

Notes: Developing Asia as defined by ADB. Figures are based on ADB estimates except for world GDP growth.

Sources: Asian Development Outlook database (accessed December 2023); and International Monetary Fund. 2023. *World Economic Outlook: Navigating Global Divergences.* Washington, DC (October).

GDP Growth in Developing Asia (%, annual)

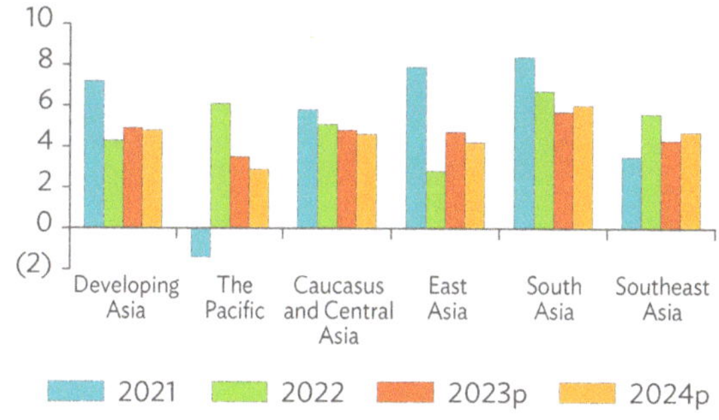

( ) = negative, p = projection.

Note: Developing Asia comprises the 46 members of the Asian Development Bank.

Source: Asian Development Outlook database (accessed December 2023)

GDP Growth in Australia and New Zealand (%, annual)

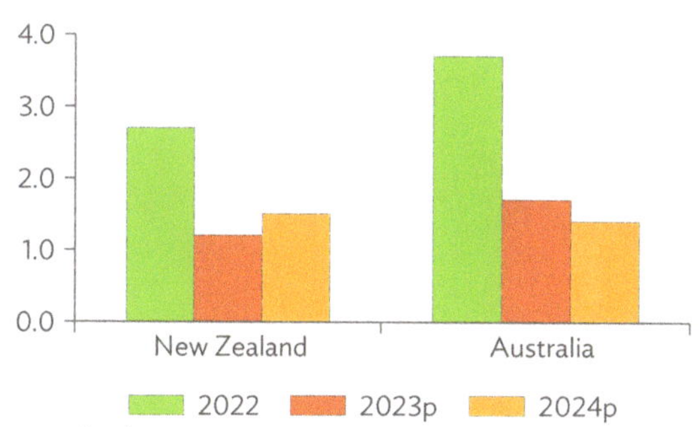

p = projection.

Source: Consensus Economics. 2023. *Asia Pacific Consensus Forecasts November 2023.* London.

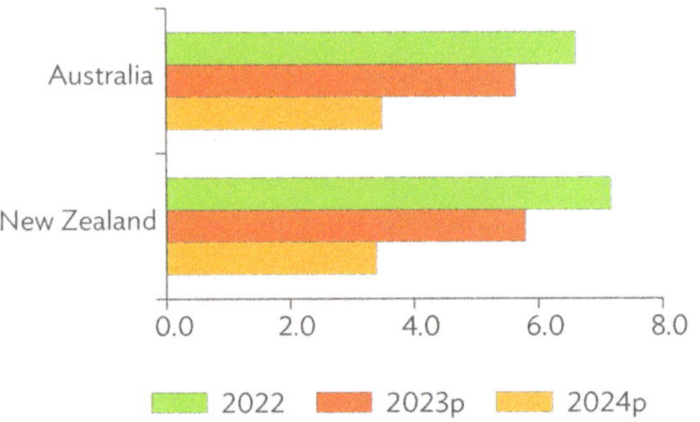

Inflation in Australia and New Zealand
(%, annual)

p = projection.
Source: Consensus Economics. 2023. *Asia Pacific Consensus Forecasts November 2023*. London.

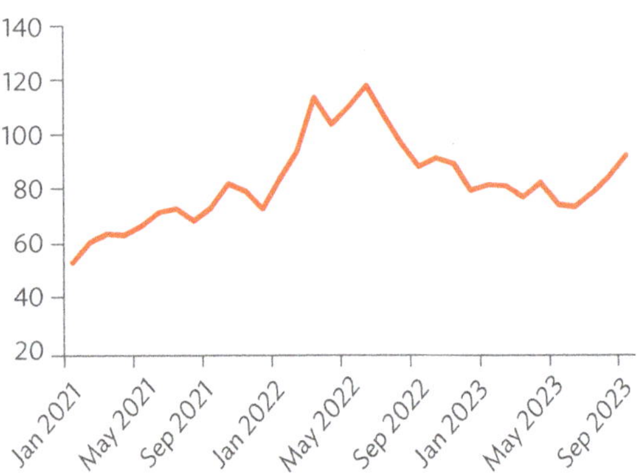

Average Spot Price of Brent Crude Oil
(monthly, $/barrel)

Source: World Bank. 2023. *World Bank Commodity Price Data* (Pink Sheet) (accessed 21 October 2023).

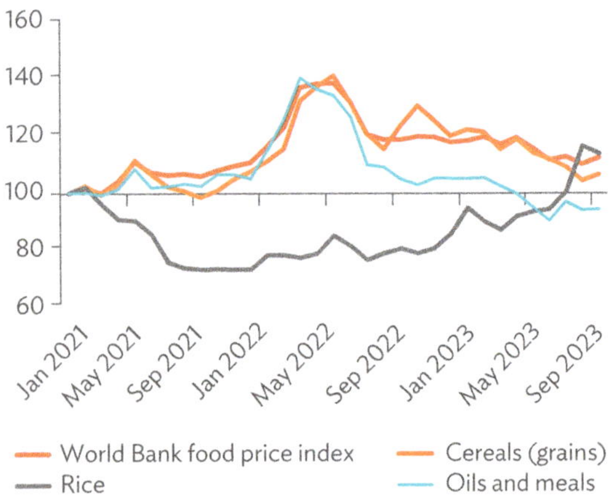

Food Prices
(January 2021 = 100)

Source: ADB calculations using data from World Bank. 2023. *World Bank Commodity Price Data* (Pink Sheet) (accessed 21 October 2023).

- Growth in the US has been resilient, accelerating to 5.2% in the third quarter (Q3) compared to the 2.1% expansion in Q2 2023. Domestic demand has remained strong with consumption holding up despite the rise in interest rates. Consumption increased by 3.6% in Q3 compared to the 0.8% growth in Q2. Meanwhile, investment and government spending also increased by 10.5% and 5.5% respectively. However, consumption growth is likely to moderate after Q3 2023 as pent-up demand wanes and excess savings from the pandemic dissipate. The prospect of "higher-for-longer" interest rates will also weigh on consumption and investment, particularly in the residential sector. The US economy is expected to grow markedly faster than earlier forecast at 2.4% for 2023 and 1.8% for 2024. Financial stability risks have receded since Q1 and the risks to the outlook have become more balanced, largely depending on the path of inflation and further adjustments by the US Federal Reserve. Inflation is forecast at 4.0% in 2023 and 2.4% in 2024.

- The lifting of pandemic-related restrictions in December 2022 and favorable base effects boosted the economy of the PRC in the first half of 2023 to 5.5% from 2.5% during the same period in 2022. Growth of 4.9% in Q3 was also stronger than expected. Economic activity was driven by a recovery in consumption and supported by growth in investment despite the downturn in the real estate sector. Slowing global demand, however, dented exports. Forecasts are revised up to 5.2% for 2023 and are unchanged at 4.5% for 2024. Domestic risks to the outlook include the possibility that accommodative fiscal and monetary policies fail to prop up growth and that a deterioration in the property sector could trigger financial instability and further weigh on economic activity. Externally, the Russian invasion of Ukraine continues to pose challenges for energy and food security; and the fragmentation of the global economy along geopolitical lines could further dampen manufacturing and exports.

- After expanding at an annualized rate of 4.8% in Q2 2023, the Japanese economy shrank by 2.1% in Q3. Growth in the first half of the year was driven by the continued recovery from the pandemic as Japan reopened its borders and supply chain disruptions dissipated. Surges in exports of automobiles and inbound tourism contributed to economic growth while imports declined as pent-up demand from the pandemic waned. However, domestic spending started to stall in Q2 as private consumption and investment growth slowed and eventually declined in Q3. Gross domestic product (GDP) is now forecast to grow by 1.6% in 2023 and 0.6% in 2024. While benefiting exporters, a weaker yen undermines consumer confidence and contributes to inflation which has remained above the Bank of Japan's 2.0% target. Moreover, an expected moderation in exports and weaker external demand could delay a recovery in capital spending.

- Growth in the Australian economy slowed to 2.1% in Q2 2023 compared to 2.4% in the previous quarter. Capital investment and services exports supported the economy through public infrastructure spending, private spending on durable goods, and robust international arrivals. Merchandise exports were also higher in Q2, with minerals benefiting from improved weather and eased supply chains. Economic activity is expected to be subdued for the rest of 2023. This reflects slower household spending due to higher interest rates, cost-of-living pressures, and capacity constraints, particularly in the labor market that weighs on construction activity. GDP is forecast to grow by 1.7% in 2023 and 1.4% in 2024.

Prices of Selected Resource Export Commodities
(January 2021 = 100)

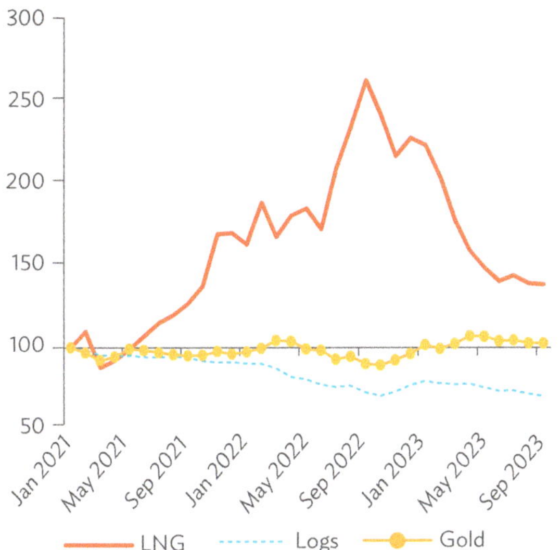

LNG = liquefied natural gas.

Source: ADB calculations using data from World Bank.
2023. *World Bank Commodity Price Data* (Pink Sheet)
(accessed 21 October 2023).

Prices of Selected Agricultural Export Commodities
(January 2021 = 100)

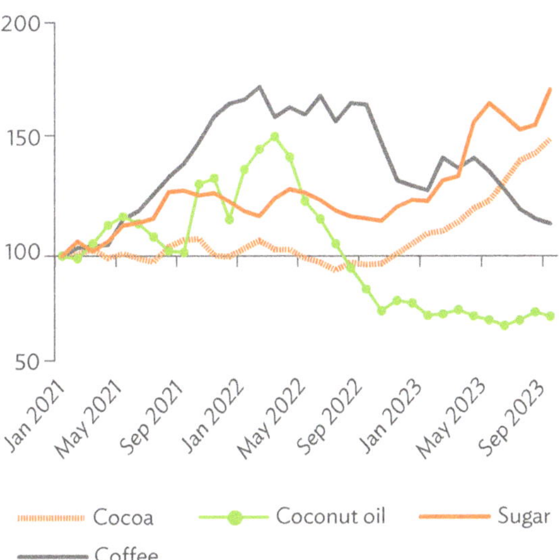

Source: ADB calculations using data from World Bank.
2023. *World Bank Commodity Price Data* (Pink Sheet)
(accessed 21 October 2023).

- Growth in New Zealand at a seasonally adjusted rate is projected to be 0.9% in Q2 2023, driven by higher exports and household spending. Dairy, forestry, and meat products led export shipments while households increased their purchases of consumer durables such as motor vehicles and audiovisual equipment. On the supply side, business services contributed the most to overall GDP growth during the quarter along with other key service subsectors. Expansion in transport equipment and machinery reversed five consecutive quarters of decline in manufacturing activity. Full-year growth is seen at 1.2% for 2023 and 1.5% for 2024. Factors negatively affecting the outlook include lower external demand; the impact of high interest rates on household wealth, consumption, and investment; and a declining share of government spending over the near- to medium-term.

Commodity prices at risk from supply issues and geopolitical concerns

- The average price of Brent crude oil was $86.80 per barrel in Q3 2023, 10.9% higher than in Q2. Driving the increase were high demand from the PRC, as well as growing concerns about tighter supply following announcements that Saudi Arabia and the Russian Federation will extend their oil production cuts until the end of 2024. From almost $100 per barrel in 2022, the average price of Brent crude oil is still forecast to moderate to $84 per barrel in 2023. Brent crude oil prices are expected to increase slightly in 2024 as geopolitical tensions in the Middle East continue, thereby prolonging supply constraints.

- The World Bank food price index declined over the first three quarters of 2023. Grain prices fell by 7.2% (quarter-on-quarter [q-o-q]) in Q3 2023—although they were still 20.0% above 2015–2019 averages—as supply increased despite the termination of the Black Sea Grain Initiative that facilitated exports from Ukraine. Prices of edible oils and oilseeds remained stable, edging up by only 0.1%, during the same quarter. Rice prices have risen throughout the year and suddenly increased by 18.2% in Q3 2023 after India—the world's biggest rice exporter—announced in July that it would expand export restrictions to secure domestic supply and stabilize local prices. Food prices are projected to decline by 9.0% in 2023 and 2.0% in 2024, already accounting for moderate to strong impacts from El Niño and rice and sugar export restrictions as well as continued favorable grain and oilseed output. Price pressures could come from heightened geopolitical conflicts, which would increase the costs of production and transportation.

- Liquefied natural gas (LNG) prices have continued to decline as global supplies remained stable despite lower production in the Russian Federation. Contract prices of LNG in Japan dipped by 6.0% (q-o-q) in Q3 2023 following a sudden drop of 25.9% in the previous quarter. This benchmark is forecast to drop by 23.9% in 2023 and 7.1% in 2024. Gold prices likewise declined by 2.5% in Q3 2023. A strong US dollar and expectations that interest rates will remain high for some time dampened the demand for gold. For 2023 as a whole, the gold price is seen to remain unchanged from 2022 but is expected to increase by 5.6% in 2024. An escalation in conflicts in the Middle East could, however, drive up prices further.

- Lower prices (q-o-q) were also observed for coffee (14.2%), logs (5.0%), and sugar (0.3%) in Q3 2023, while prices rose for cocoa (15.9%) and coconut oil (2.7%) during the period. Despite the slight decline, sugar prices are still expected to be higher in 2023 than in 2022 because of continued demand from the PRC as well as an export ban from India, then may moderate in

Tourist Departures for Pacific Destinations
('000 persons, January to August totals)

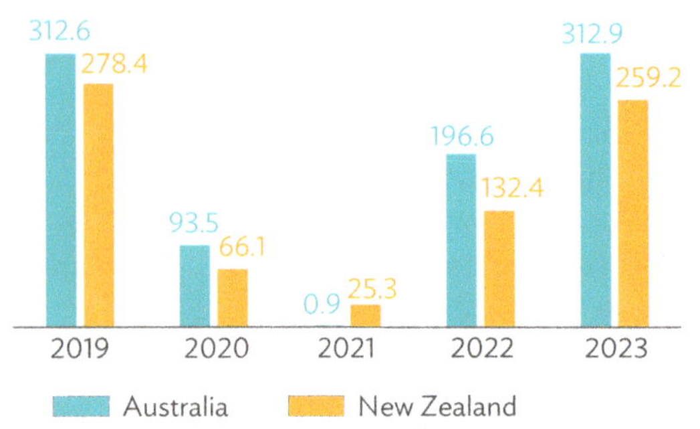

Sources: Government of Australia, Australian Bureau of Statistics. Overseas Arrivals and Departures (accessed 21 October 2023), and Government of New Zealand, Stats NZ Tatauranga Aotearoa: International Travel and Migration (accessed 21 October 2023).

Outbound Tourism from Major Source Markets
(relative to pre–COVID-19 pandemic levels, monthly)

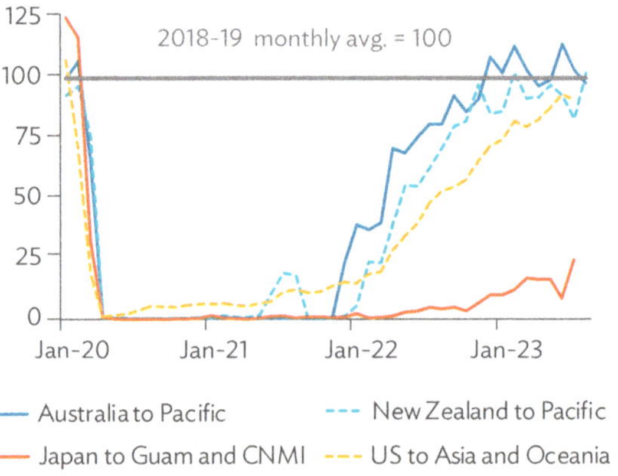

avg. = average, CNMI = Commonwealth of the Northern Mariana Islands, COVID-19 = coronavirus disease, US = United States.

Sources: Government of Australia, Bureau of Statistics. Overseas Arrivals and Departures (accessed 21 October 2023), Japan Tourism Marketing Co. Japanese Outbound Tourists Statistics (accessed 21 October 2023), Government of New Zealand, Stats NZ Tatauranga Aotearoa: International Travel and Migration (accessed 21 October 2023), and Government of the US, Department of Commerce International Trade Administration: US Outbound Travel to World Regions (accessed 21 October 2023).

Lead authors: Remrick Patagan and Cara Tinio.

2024 as global production increases. Similar trends are seen for cocoa prices because of supply movements. The price of coffee is projected to drop in 2023 and decline further in 2024. Prices of coconut oil and logs are expected to fall in 2023 but increase in 2024.

Recovery in tourism to the Pacific remains uneven

- Visitor arrivals to the South Pacific continue to recover as outbound travel from Australia and New Zealand—the main source markets for the subregion—remain strong. In January–August 2023, there were 248,870 visitors to Fiji, 111.4% of the 2018–2019 average for the same period. Similarly, Australian visitors to Samoa in the first 8 months of 2023 numbered 24,880, 113.9% of 2018–2019 levels, while those to Vanuatu were 32,350 (107.6%). However, the number of Australian visitors to the Cook Islands (6,256) was equivalent to just 49.1% of pre-pandemic levels, and the visitors to Tonga (5,274) was 59.9%.

- Departures from New Zealand to the South Pacific were 92.4% of pre-pandemic levels. Visitors to Fiji in the first 8 months of 2023 totaled 133,071, 101.4% of the average for the same months in 2018–2019, the only South Pacific destination to surpass this benchmark. Tourism to Samoa, with 42,912 visitors in the same period, is catching up at 91.9%. Departures to the Cook Islands and Tonga—totaling 59,450 and 16,170 visitors, respectively—averaged 82.0% of their pre-pandemic levels during the period, while New Zealand tourism to Vanuatu remained relatively weak at 7,560 visitors, equivalent to 62.5% of pre-pandemic tourist numbers.

- Lags in tourism recovery to some South Pacific destinations partly reflect ongoing issues regarding the availability of flights and/or accommodations. The twin cyclones that hit Vanuatu in March 2023 disrupted flights and caused widespread physical damage, while the impacts of the January 2022 volcanic eruption and tsunami linger in Tonga.

- In the North Pacific, recovery in visitor arrivals to Palau remains uneven. Outbound travel from the US is on a generally upward trend and catching up to pre-pandemic levels. In contrast, data from Japan show that tourism from this source market is still weak; it averaged 15.1% of pre-pandemic arrivals during January–July 2023.

References

Consensus Economics. 2023. *Asia Pacific Consensus Forecasts November 2023*. London.

Government of Australia, Bureau of Statistics. 2023. Australian National Accounts: National Income, Expenditure and Product. *Media release.* 6 September.

Government of New Zealand, Stats NZ Tatauranga Aotearoa. 2023. Gross domestic product: June 2023 quarter. *Media release.* 21 September.

International Monetary Fund. 2023. *World Economic Outlook: Navigating Global Divergences.* Washington, DC (October).

E. Manthey. 2023. Higher-for-longer rates narrative takes the shine off gold. *ING Think.* 5 October.

World Bank. 2023. *Commodity Markets Outlook: Under the Shadow of Geopolitical Risks, October 2023.* Washington, DC.

COUNTRY ECONOMIC ISSUES

Domestic resource mobilization (DRM) is the process wherein governments raise resources required to deliver infrastructure and public services essential for achieving poverty alleviation and economic growth objectives. In addition to setting tax rates, DRM involves simplified tax filing, administration, and audit procedures that can also improve transparency, governance, and the business climate in a country.

DRM is challenging in many Pacific developing member countries (DMCs), with their narrow economic bases and implementation capacity constraints. Pacific DMCs also face a pressing need to stabilize their fiscal positions and support their economies in restoring development gains lost during the coronavirus disease pandemic amid continued vulnerability to climate change and disasters.

Tax revenue management in practice: Lessons from the Cook Islands

Lead author: Lily-Anne Homasi

Pacific DMCs, including the Cook Islands, face overwhelming spending needs to support social services, infrastructure investments, and climate change adaptation. Because of limited financing options, boosting tax revenues has been an essential pillar of the Cook Islands' strategy to create fiscal space to meet these requirements and drive economic growth. The Cook Islands is one of the best-performing economies in the Pacific when it comes to tax administration. Taxes generate over 70% of domestic revenues, averaging NZ$125 million annually which is equivalent to more than 26% of gross domestic product (GDP) in the last 5 years (2018–2022). The Cook Islands' tax-to-GDP ratio in 2021 was 7.1 percentage points higher than the 19.8% average for Asia and the Pacific (OECD 2023a). Key contributors were value-added taxes (VAT) and personal income taxes. Notwithstanding these successes, skilled labor shortages and capacity constraints continue to hamper inland revenue activities. This article highlights aspects of the Cook Islands' success and challenges, paving the way forward for an improved revenue management regime to support economic recovery.

UNDERSTANDING THE CONTEXT

Among Pacific DMCs, the Cook Islands economy was the hardest hit by the COVID-19 pandemic, with GDP contracting by an estimated 15.7% in fiscal year 2020 (FY2020, ended 30 June) and 25.5% in FY2021. The economy bounced back after the reopening of borders in January 2022, but the downturn had a severe impact on tax revenue. Targeted and concerted efforts by the government helped to curb economic losses from the pandemic, and sustained support from stakeholders will be critical for a strong and inclusive economic recovery. In particular, the large and comprehensive economic response packages helped employers (the private sector) retain their staff and contribute income tax and VAT to the government. This moderated the impact of the downturn on domestic revenues.

The government receives revenue through three main sources: taxes on businesses and individuals; funding from development partners; and other sources such as fees, licenses, dividends, and trading revenue (Figure 1). Taxation brings in the highest amount of consistent revenue of the three revenue streams, with the second-highest source typically being aid funding, which takes the form of cash and contributions to government operations. The other revenue consists of agency trading revenue, various fees, miscellaneous cash flows, and licensing costs. For FY2024, the government forecasts that tax revenue will increase by 25% from FY2023 levels driven by ongoing tax reforms, and grants by 260% driven by New Zealand's commitment over FY2024 and FY2025 for various programs, including the Cook Islands Core Sector Support, Budget Support toward Economic Recovery, Information and Communication Technology (ICT) Connectivity Improvements, Climate Finance Facility, and the Cook Islands Infrastructure Fund for capital projects (Government of the Cook Islands, Ministry of Finance and Economic Management 2023).

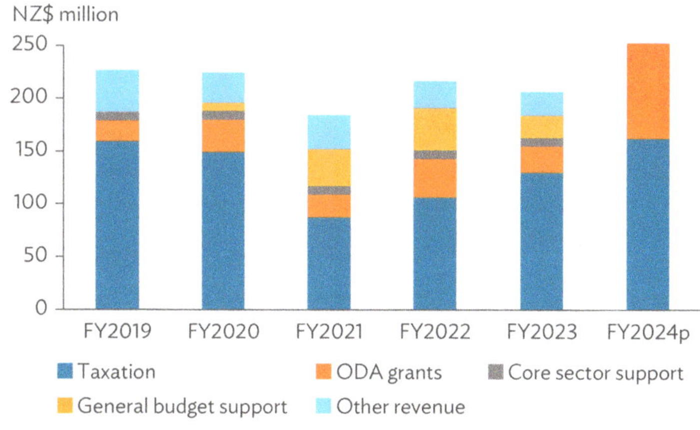

Figure 1: Cook Islands Revenue Composition by Source

FY = fiscal year, NZ$ = New Zealand dollar, ODA = official development assistance, p = projection.

Note: The fiscal year of the Government of the Cook Islands ends on 30 June.

Source: Government of the Cook Islands. National Budget Estimates, 6 years (FY2019–FY2024).

MEASURES INSTITUTED TO SUPPORT REVENUE MANAGEMENT

Up-to-date legal framework to drive revenue management. Several laws drive the Cook Islands' revenue management work. The main one—the Income Tax Act 1997—has been amended several times to respond to changes in the economic environment. The latest amendment came into effect on 1 July 2023. This Act provides the legal framework for income tax administration in the Cook Islands, including the role of the Revenue Management Division (RMD) in assessing and pursuing individual and business tax obligations under the law. The act, regulations, and charter provide the RMD with the mandate to collect taxes from eligible individuals and businesses, which support critical core services such as social services for Cook Islanders and visitors to the country.

Dedicated Revenue Management Division equipped with support services. The RMD, which is part of the Ministry of Finance and Economic Management, has four main units, including Inland Revenue. Within the inland revenue unit, there are four separate teams: taxpayer services, income tax, value-added tax, and collections and international support. The RMD has a dedicated administrative function in human resources, legal services, ICT, communications, and finance. It also has a design and monitoring team leading the design and implementation of RMD-wide compliance improvement strategies for inland revenue and customs services and monitoring overall tax compliance. These teams are critical for providing tax education and awareness, assessment, and audits to get a clearer understanding of the status of each tax return and its contribution to tax revenue in the country.

Web-based tax registration and filing system facilitating timely filing and assessment of tax returns. The web-based eTax taxation system—which commenced operations during the COVID-19 pandemic—compensated for labor shortages in the country and allowed taxpayers to register and file their tax returns remotely. The system provides real-time interaction between the public and the RMD. The web page also provides direct phone and email contacts for customers to submit their queries. The updated tax system created efficiencies, reducing compliance costs and improving customer services. This is a critical area that other smaller Pacific Island countries struggle with, but that technology could address.

Timely updates of standard operating procedures (SOPs) to support work. During the COVID-19 pandemic, the RMD revised and updated 26 SOPs for key business processes across collections (debt and returns), audits, and taxpayer services. This was critical during the pandemic to be more agile amid the changing operating environment. This work helped the RMD contribute to administering economic response package measures with over 30,000 reviews of applications completed during 2020–2021.

Increased transparency of taxation in line with Global Forum membership. For a small island nation, the Cook Islands' revenue management processes are comprehensive and transparent, with most of the information regarding tax filing publicly available. The Cook Islands is one of three Pacific Island countries that are members of the Organisation for Economic Co-operation and Development's (OECD) Inclusive Framework on Base Erosion and Profit Shifting (OECD 2023c). The framework emphasizes equipping governments with domestic and international rules and instruments to address tax avoidance, ensuring that profits are taxed where economic activities generating the profits are performed and where value is created. The international section of the inland revenue unit operates the RMD Common Reporting Standard web portal that collects and monitors account information filed by financial institutions, then collates and exchanges information for tax purposes in a secure and timely manner. Besides helping to build the Cook Islands' international profile, participating in these international forums increases its exposure to new and improved ways and tools for enhancing tax reporting transparency and revenue management. This, in turn, leads to increased tax revenues.

CHALLENGES AND OPPORTUNITIES

The lack of a medium-term revenue management strategy or roadmap presents an opportunity for future strategic work. The RMD recognizes that this is an area that could further strengthen its role, better communicate its targets, and identify how these will be resourced through government and external support. Although the Ministry of Finance and Economic Management Strategic Plan 2022–2026 provides the strategic direction for agencies under its mandate, the RMD could benefit from a streamlined revenue management strategy or roadmap that, among other things, determines its targets, performance indicators, human resource requirements, and other technological improvements to further improve the digitalization of tax administration in the Cook Islands. This aligns with advice from the International Monetary Fund (IMF) (Sy et al. 2022).

Labor shortages and opportunities to consolidate common functions to elevate the current work. While it is critical to have support services as part of the RMD, labor migration is a reality in the Cook Islands. A review can identify which functions under the division could be best housed elsewhere within the government's centralized structure, particularly common functions such as human resources, ICT, and legal services. The government has embarked on a functional review to realign the workforce with the current and future needs and aspirations of the nation. Findings from the review could help reduce any overlaps and increase the pool of common cadre functions made available to the RMD as well as other government agencies as a way of streamlining functions, addressing the labor shortage issues, and further strengthening support services for the RMD.

Use of artificial intelligence (AI) technology to boost taxpayer services. AI is still a new area for the Pacific and needs to be cautiously employed. To further strengthen taxpayer services, the use of AI technology could be a useful solution to labor shortages and improve the timeliness of advisory services and support provided. The eTax system could integrate such technology as a functionality to reduce staff time in actively managing the platform. However, this would need to be explored systematically and supported with SOPs to ensure that confidentiality and privacy issues are managed.

Figure 2: Cook Islands Revenue Composition by Tax Types

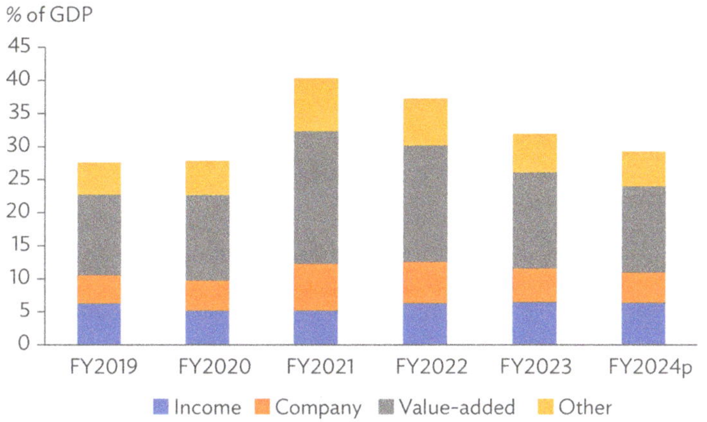

FY = fiscal year, GDP = gross domestic product, p = projection.
Note: The fiscal year of the Government of the Cook Islands ends on 30 June.
Source: Government of the Cook Islands. National Budget Estimates. Rarotonga (6 years: FY2019–FY2024).

Reforming VAT systems. Although VAT is one of the best-performing tax types in the Cook Islands, the government is not fully exploiting the potential offered by efficient VAT systems (Figure 2). A good VAT system has many advantages including reducing noncompliance and boosting non-VAT taxes. According to the IMF (Sy et al. 2022), in the Pacific subregion low VAT rates, widespread VAT tax exemptions, and zero ratings result in an average gap of about 50% between current and potential VAT collections. Technical assistance and advice from development partners and experts could further explore and support this.

THE WAY FORWARD

The Cook Islands showcases how a small administration was able to deliver comprehensive taxpayer services through online tax registration, filing and assessment of tax returns, and facilitating the collection of tax revenues. The RMD has instituted reforms providing efficient and effective revenue management in practice, leading to an immense contribution to government revenues.

The experience of the Cook Islands offers a roadmap for neighboring countries that face tax administration issues. This article also highlights existing challenges and opportunities for the Cook Islands to consider, including developing a medium-term revenue management strategy, consolidating common functions to mitigate labor shortages experienced in the country, exploring AI in its business operations, and further strengthening VAT systems. Development partner support will be critical in the Cook Islands' efforts and reforms to strengthen revenue management for improved taxation revenues and service delivery.

References

Asian Development Bank (ADB). Asian Development Outlook Database for Cook Islands (accessed 13 November 2023).

Government of the Cook Islands, Ministry of Finance and Economic Management (MFEM). 2022. Strategic Plan 2022–26. Rarotonga.

Government of the Cook Islands, MFEM. 2023. National Budget Estimates 2023–2024. Rarotonga.

Government of the Cook Islands, MFEM. Revenue Management Division.

M. Sy et al. 2022. Funding the Future: Tax Mobilization in Pacific Island Countries. *Departmental Paper No. 2022/015*. Washington, DC: IMF.

Organisation for Economic Co-operation and Development (OECD). 2023a. *Revenue Statistics in Asia and the Pacific 2023*.

OECD. 2023b. Member of the OECD/G20 Inclusive Framework on Base Erosion and Profit Shifting (BEPS).

OECD. 2023c. BEPS Actions - OECD BEPS (accessed 3 November 2023).

The continuing journey toward fiscal self-sufficiency in the North Pacific

Lead authors: Remrick Patagan and Cara Tinio, with contributions from Maybelline Andon-Bing

Development assistance received under their Compacts of Free Association with the United States (US) has shored up the fiscal positions of the Federated States of Micronesia (FSM), the Marshall Islands, and Palau for decades. Although the assistance has declined over time as stipulated in the agreements, the reliability of this resource inflow—coupled with the increased significance of certain nontax revenue streams such as fishing license fees—has reduced incentives for North Pacific governments to mobilize domestic fiscal resources.

As of October 2023, all three North Pacific economies had signed agreements with the US to extend their respective compacts. This will provide the FSM, the Marshall Islands, and Palau with additional time to pursue public financial management (PFM) reforms, including improvements to tax collection. This write-up explores the challenges to—and progress thus far—in broadening revenue bases and enhancing tax system efficiency to help ensure fiscal self-sufficiency in the North Pacific.

FEDERATED STATES OF MICRONESIA

Since 2012, the Government of the Federated States of Micronesia has posted significant fiscal surpluses that peaked at about 24.3% of GDP in FY2018 (ended on 30 September for all three North

Pacific economies) when tax revenue reached a historic high of $99.4 million, largely due to one-off capital gains payments by major corporations. Tax collections constitute a relatively low proportion of domestic and total revenues in the FSM, overshadowed by external grant funding and fishing license fees in FY2020 and FY2021 (Figure 3).

Figure 3: Federated States of Micronesia Revenue Sources

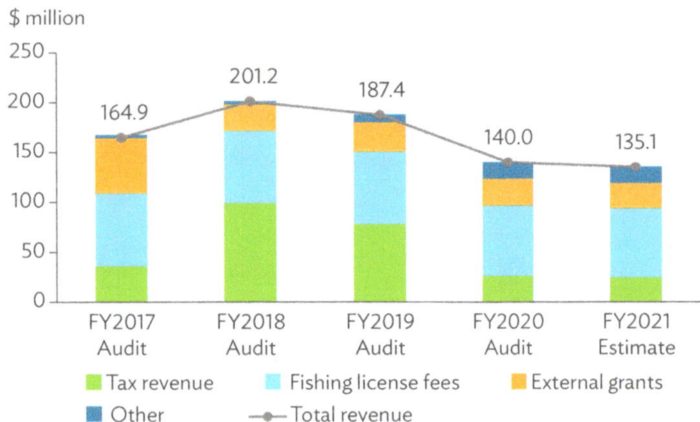

FY = fiscal year.

Note: The fiscal year of the Government of the Federated States of Micronesia ends on 30 September.

Source: Government of the Federated States of Micronesia. 2022. FSM Economic and Fiscal Update 2022.

The FSM remains heavily dependent on development assistance, particularly from the US, which provides grant financing for major public services such as education, health, and infrastructure. Under the compact, the US also makes contributions to the FSM Compact Trust Fund (CTF), which is expected to help finance public expenses once grant funding ends. To further augment fiscal buffers, the Government of the Federated States of Micronesia created a separate FSM Trust Fund (FTF), which receives 50% of corporate income tax revenues and 20% of fishing license fee collections. An estimated CTF value of $2.74 billion is needed to sustainably finance public expenditure requirements compared to actual CTF assets of $999.8 million and FTF assets of $370.9 million as of FY2021 (Figure 4).

In early 2023, the governments of the FSM and the US signed a memorandum of understanding on the renewal and extension of the compact through to 2044. While this development bolsters the Government of the Federated States of Micronesia's revenue prospects, achieving fiscal sustainability remains an ongoing challenge. Contributions to domestic revenue from fishing license fees have stabilized at about $70 million but the long-term outlook is clouded by the impact of climate change on FSM offshore fisheries (Patagan 2022). Even as the government expects tax revenue to grow annually by 2% in line with projected economic growth, this will be a challenge considering annual average growth was less than 1% in the decade before the pandemic. Fiscal performance also influences the CTF and FTF through expenditure requirements and fund contributions.

Figure 4: Net Assets of the FSM Compact Trust Fund and FSM Trust Fund

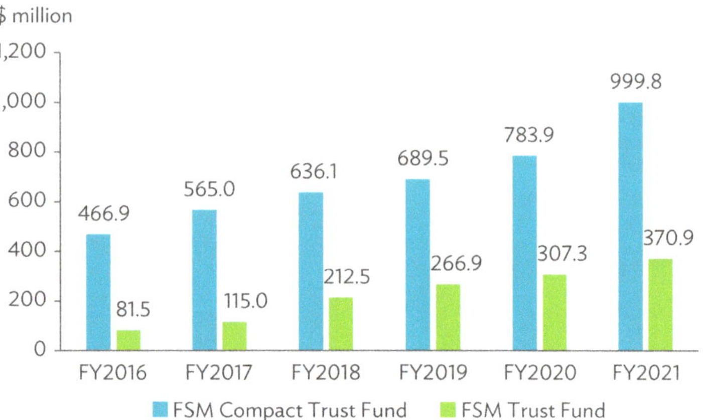

FSM = Federated States of Micronesia, FY = fiscal year.

Note: The fiscal year of the Government of the Federated States of Micronesia ends on 30 September.

Source: Government of the Federated States of Micronesia. 2022. FSM Economic and Fiscal Update 2022.

The risk of fiscal deterioration is illustrated by the FSM's experience during the pandemic. The national government entered the crisis with a strong fiscal position, bolstered by revenues from fishing license fees and offshore corporate tax payments. However, the COVID-19 shock significantly reduced tax revenue while increasing demand for public spending. Consequently, the fiscal surplus declined sharply in FY2020 and FY2021 (Figure 5). Moreover, tax revenue as a percentage of GDP remains low by international standards averaging 13.4% during FY2017–FY2021 compared to an average of 20% for the Pacific subregion.

Figure 5: Federated States of Micronesia Fiscal Balance

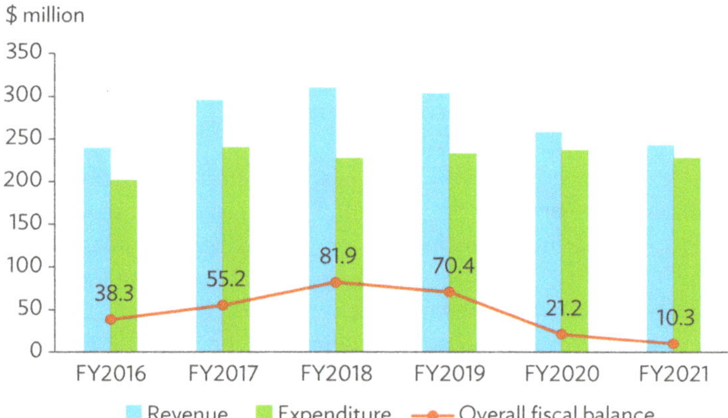

FY = fiscal year.

Note: The fiscal year of the Government of the Federated States of Micronesia ends on 30 September.

Source: ADB estimates.

The government acknowledges the importance of domestic revenue mobilization to ensure the sustainability of public finances. It also notes that careful planning is needed to avoid adverse impacts on economic growth given the outsized role of the public sector in the economy. The government's fiscal strategy broadly rests on the two prongs of comprehensive PFM and tax reforms which taken together aim to raise the tax revenue-to-GDP ratio to 16.0% in the medium term.

The PFM Reform Roadmap 2023–2026—which was launched in January 2023—includes the implementation of an automated revenue management system and Automated Systems for Customs Data (ASYCUDA); a new financial management information system (FMIS); updates to budget and financial management regulations and internal procedures; and payments system modernization. A similar tax reform roadmap is being developed by a national Tax Reform Commission. The government plans for a phased implementation of tax reforms in succeeding years involving the adoption of a VAT system, a new net profits tax to replace the current gross receipts tax on business income, an increase in "sin" taxes on alcohol, tobacco, and sugary beverages, as well as exploring other possible revenue sources. The final form of the tax reform package will depend on the modeling of projected outcomes, which is still ongoing.

The FSM's ambitious and wide-ranging domestic resource mobilization (DRM) reform efforts are noteworthy and deserve full support from all stakeholders. However, the comprehensiveness of the reform effort may also present a challenge to successful implementation, especially considering the long-standing capacity constraints in the public sector and the need for effective coordination between national and state governments. A proper sequencing of reforms must be based on a clear-eyed assessment of what the government aims to achieve and what can be realistically done within given time frames. Aside from tax reforms—scheduled in late FY2026—the PFM roadmap has 8 expected outcomes and 12 key reform areas.[1] It could benefit from further prioritization of the expected outcomes and closely linking them with necessary reforms. In addition, the importance of timely and sufficient change management and capacity-building cannot be overemphasized. There is scope in these areas for further support from development partners.

MARSHALL ISLANDS

Except for small deficits during FY2012–FY2013 and FY2019, the Marshall Islands realized fiscal surpluses during FY2010–FY2021. Compact grants lifted the budget position along with increased revenues from fishing license fees after the Parties to the Nauru Agreement fully implemented the vessel day scheme (Figure 6).

As percentages of GDP, compact grants declined from 20.6% in FY2012 to 15.1% in FY2021 in keeping with planned decrements under the agreement, while fishing license fees rose from 2.3% to a peak of 18.8% in FY2017 before declining to 10.0% by FY2021 (Figure 7). During the same period, tax revenues did not deviate significantly from an average of 14.4% of GDP.

Economic growth contributed to increased tax collections, but reform efforts were unable to maintain this performance when expansion faltered. Tax collections declined from a decade high

of 15.0% of GDP in FY2019 to 13.8% in FY2021 as the COVID-19 pandemic affected economic activity. There is anecdotal evidence that tax collections were already low even before the impacts of the COVID-19 pandemic were felt (ADB 2020).

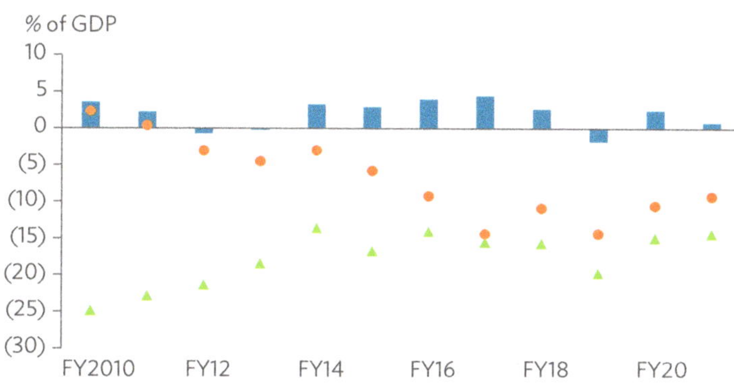

Figure 6: Marshall Islands Fiscal Balance

( ) = negative, FY = fiscal year, GDP = gross domestic product, US = United States.
Note: The fiscal year of the Government of the Marshall Islands ends on 30 September.
Source: ADB estimates based on Graduate School USA. 2022. Fiscal Year 2021 Economic Statistics (Preliminary).

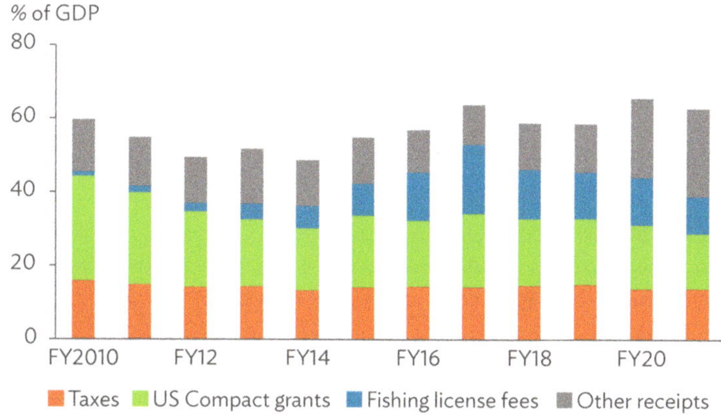

Figure 7: Marshall Islands Revenue Performance

FY = fiscal year, GDP = gross domestic product, US = United States.
Note: The fiscal year of the Government of the Marshall Islands ends on 30 September.
Source: ADB estimates based on Graduate School USA. 2022. Fiscal Year 2021 Economic Statistics (Preliminary).

Rather than directly pursuing legislative reforms envisioned to increase revenues, the Government of the Marshall Islands is focusing first on improving its administration systems. One key challenge is the need to automate revenue collection and management procedures, which would help reduce clerical error and enable more accurate and timely reporting. It would also ease the time burden on taxpayers and enable concerned government personnel to devote more effort to ensuring tax compliance (ADB

2020, ADB 2021b). Data arising from automation could help the government identify tax compliance risks and inform strategies to mitigate these.

The government has begun implementing a new FMIS and is adopting an ASYCUDA system (IMF 2023). When fully implemented, an FMIS can help boost DRM by monitoring the trends in tax revenues, debt stock and tracking revenue collections against targets. ASYCUDA systems help make customs revenue collection more accurate and efficient and improve the monitoring of trade activity, which should provide useful information in a highly import-dependent economy such as the Marshall Islands.

On 17 October 2023, the governments of the Marshall Islands and the US agreed to renew their Compact of Free Association. Given that the parties' respective legislatures need to ratify the agreement for it to take effect, the timing of its implementation—including the continued provision of development assistance—remains uncertain as of November 2023. Drawdowns from the Marshall Island CTF— which was established to offset expired compact grants—may not fill this gap (Tinio 2022, IMF 2023). Meanwhile, higher international prices, the increased likelihood of disasters, and more severe impacts of climate change contribute to the expectation of greater financing needs in the near- to medium-term. Even with the additional leeway under a renewed compact, domestic revenue mobilization remains an urgent need.

Although the Marshall Islands is still in the early stages of automating its revenue systems, this provides a strong foundation for further reforms to strengthen tax administration and DRM. Other measures under consideration include improving the government's taxpayer outreach and audit functions, as well as the introduction of new taxes.

PALAU

Palau followed sound fiscal management policies that resulted in consistent fiscal surpluses before the pandemic. Previous reforms that raised tobacco and departure taxes increased the country's tax-to-GDP ratio to an average of 20.2% during FY2015–FY2019 from 17.3% during FY2005–FY2014. At the same time, the government also successfully controlled the public sector wage bill which declined to an average of 14.7% during FY2015–FY2019 from 17.1% during FY2005–FY2014. These efforts led to an average annual fiscal surplus of 3.0% during FY2011–FY2019. Sustained surpluses built up government deposits to the general fund reserve, which was established in FY2014 as a fiscal buffer to be drawn on during times of need (ADB 2021a).

COVID-19 severely affected Palau's tourism-dependent economy. A rise in external grant funding, notably from the US, only partly offset considerable declines in tax revenue (Figure 8). However, public expenditure drastically increased and fiscal surpluses were replaced by a deficit equivalent to 6.7% of GDP in FY2020. While figures have improved since FY2021–FY2023, the government's fiscal position in FY2023–FY2024 is not yet expected to recover to their pre-pandemic levels.

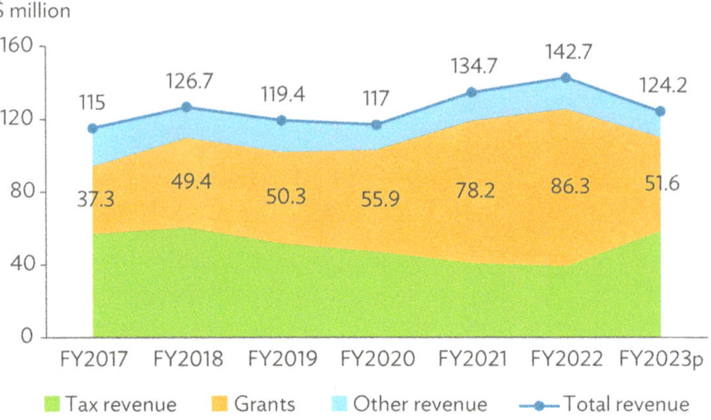

Figure 8: Palau Revenues

FY = fiscal year, p = preliminary.
Note: The fiscal year of the Government of Palau ends on 30 September.
Source: Government of Palau. 2023. Republic of Palau Economic and Fiscal Update FY2023.

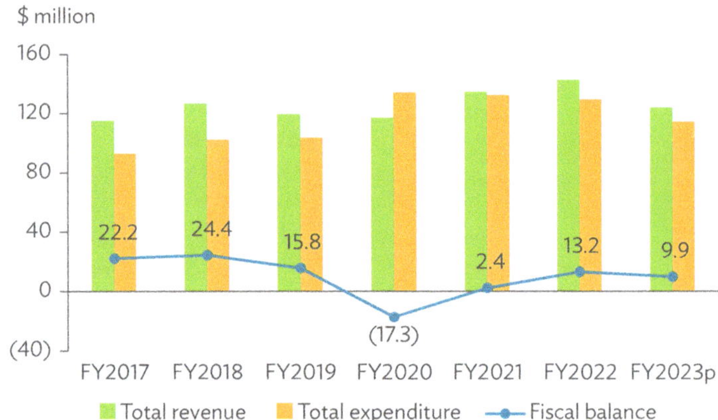

Figure 9: Palau Fiscal Balance

( ) = negative, FY = fiscal year, p = preliminary.
Note: The fiscal year of the Government of Palau ends on 30 September.
Source: Government of Palau. 2023. Republic of Palau Economic and Fiscal Update FY2023.

As with the FSM and the Marshall Islands, Palau has successfully concluded negotiations with the US on the renewal of their compact, with Congressional approval now expected in FY2024. Nevertheless, public sector reform continues to be critical to contain fiscal risks and support a sustainable post-pandemic recovery (ADB 2022). Notably, domestic revenue mobilization will have to take up the slack from the normalization of external grant funding. Moreover, the full recovery of the Palau tourism industry is uncertain (although the pace picked up during 2023) while the country remains vulnerable to external shocks to food and fuel prices as well as disasters arising from natural hazards and climate change.

Cognizant of the challenges, the Government of Palau considers tax reform a key part of its fiscal strategy. According to its Fiscal Responsibility Framework, the revenue base consisting of taxes on wages, gross receipts, and imports has declined when adjusted for inflation. This has been balanced by increased taxes on tobacco and tourist departures along with windfall gains from fishing royalties and economic growth, but the country needs sustainable alternatives to address potential fiscal imbalances.

The tax system of Palau is heavily dependent on business gross receipts taxes and import duties which comprise around half of total collections (ADB 2021). The former is levied on output and cascades with each transaction. The latter is not buoyant as it is inelastic concerning GDP. Both taxes are distortionary. Along with the lack of an effective tax on capital which makes the system inequitable, these weaknesses discourage private investment.

The government has committed to reforming the country's weak and outdated tax system and transitioning toward a modern and efficient tax regime suited to the structure of the Palau economy (Government of Palau 2021). Recent reforms—supported by ADB's Recovery through Improved Systems and Expenditure Support Program—involve the passage of a tax reform package in 2021 which was implemented at the start of 2023. This includes the following key components:

(i)   a 10% Palau Goods and Services Tax;
(ii)   a 12% Business Profits Tax;
(iii)   reductions in the wages tax for certain income levels and a tax refund for those with annual incomes below $15,000;
(iv)   conversion of specific import duties into excise taxes applied to both imported and domestic products; and
(v)   introduction of a carbon tax.

These reforms have driven a strong increase in tax revenue in FY2023 that is likely to be carried into FY2024. For instance, preliminary estimates indicate Palau Goods and Services Tax collections worth $17.2 million in FY2023 which is considerably higher than business gross receipts tax collections averaging $14.2 million during FY2017–FY2019. While the fiscal balance has reverted to a modest surplus, the recovery remains fragile giventhe economy has yet to recover from the COVID-19 shock, the delay in the implementation of the renewed Compact Agreement, and political pushback against the contribution of tax reforms to recent double-digit inflation.

Nonetheless, the government acknowledges the need to stay the course of the recent reforms and control spending. An evaluation of the tax reform initiative will seek to initiate improvements to the new system and consider the imposition of a general personal income tax. Further administrative reforms to be pursued include the modernization of the Tax Information System and customs modernization through the operationalization of ASYCUDA.

The apparent success of Palau's latest tax reform initiative, despite limited capacity, could provide lessons for neighbors in the North Pacific embarking on similar efforts. These involve the use of a programmatic approach with initial actions that lay the foundation for more substantive reforms, interim milestones to sustain momentum and maintain the government's focus on reform outputs, broad-based engagement while building capacity for deeper reforms, and integration with development partner activities to reinforce results (ADB 2021a).

CONCLUSION

Sizable inflows of development partner grants and nontax revenues in the FSM and the Marshall Islands have masked outdated taxation systems and weak tax collection and administration in the North Pacific. Even with the prospect of renewed compacts for all three economies, improving DRM remains an urgent need. The uncertainty in their main revenue sources, i.e., fisheries (for the FSM and the Marshall Islands) and tourism (for Palau), casts doubt on the sustainability of these economies' revenue bases. This is further complicated by the heightened need for fiscal resilience to the socioeconomic impacts of shocks such as increasingly frequent and severe climate change and disaster events.

To address this, the North Pacific economies are working to implement reforms to enhance administrative efficiency and accuracy such as the introduction of automated revenue collection and management systems, as well as updating and rationalizing their tax regimes. Prioritization and phasing are needed to ensure that the wide scope of actions needed to improve DRM is implemented properly despite government constraints.

Endnote

[1]   Key reform areas under the PFM Reform Roadmap involve: a new system for managing financial information; an improved approach to human resource development; new technology for enhancing customs and tax management; strengthened operational budgetary procedures; improved capacity development strategy; updated financial management regulations; strengthened public debt management; integration of environmental, social, and governance considerations into investment strategies; enhancement of drawdown procedures for Federal grants assistance; new municipality payments system; strengthened FSM Trust Fund management; and improved internal compliance.

References

Asian Development Bank (ADB). 2020. Report and Recommendation of the President to the Board of Directors: Proposed Grant to the Republic of the Marshall Islands for the Public Financial Management Project. Consultant's report. Unpublished.

ADB. 2021a. *Recovery through Improved Systems and Expenditure Support Program, Subprogram 1.* March.

ADB. 2021b. Report and Recommendation of the President to the Board of Directors: Proposed Grant to the Republic of the Marshall Islands for the Public Financial Management Project. Consultant's report. Unpublished.

ADB. 2022. *Recovery through Improved Systems and Expenditure Support Program, Subprogram 2.* August.

Government of the Federated States of Micronesia. 2022. *FSM Economic and Fiscal Update 2022*.

Government of the Federated States of Micronesia. 2023. *FSM Public Financial Management Reform Roadmap 2023–2026*.

Government of Palau. 2021. *Fiscal Responsibility Framework: Rational [sic] and Description (including Guidelines for Palau's Medium-Term Budget Cycle)*.

Government of Palau. 2023. *Republic of Palau Economic and Fiscal Update FY2023*.

Graduate School USA. 2022. *Marshall Islands Fiscal Year 2021 Economic Statistics (Preliminary)*.

International Monetary Fund. 2023. Republic of the Marshall Islands 2023 Article IV Consultation. *IMF Country Report*. No. 23/349. Washington, DC.

R. Patagan. 2022. Future-proofing fisheries in the Federated States of Micronesia. In *Pacific Economic Monitor*. December. Asian Development Bank.

C. Tinio. 2022. Pondering post-pandemic social protection in the Marshall Islands. In *Pacific Economic Monitor*. December. Asian Development Bank.

Government of the United States, Department of State. 2023. *The United States and the Republic of the Marshall Islands Sign Three Compact of Free Association-Related Agreements*.

Paying its way out of the woods: Mobilizing domestic revenue to achieve fiscal consolidation in Fiji

Lead authors: Isoa Wainiqolo and Noel Del Castillo

For the decade prior to the COVID-19 pandemic, Fiji had averaged relatively modest fiscal deficits. However, the deficit as a percentage of GDP widened substantially to 5.9% in FY2020 (ended 31 July), 11.4% in FY2021 and 11.9% in FY2022. As a result of these fiscal deficits, the debt-to-GDP ratio increased from 48.8% in FY2019 to 88.8% in FY2022. To restore fiscal sustainability, the government has rolled out a medium-term fiscal strategy for FY2024–FY2026, aiming to put the debt-to-GDP ratio on a downward path and return the revenue-to-GDP ratio to pre-pandemic levels. To do this, the government intends to widen the tax base by gradually removing exemptions; improving tax compliance and collection of tax arrears; and simplifying the tax regime and administration. The IMF 2023 Article IV report suggested that fiscal consolidation should lean toward a comprehensive and growth-friendly tax reform strategy such as unifying and increasing value-added tax (VAT) rates, raising the corporate income tax rate, raising the departure tax, and reducing tax exemptions for corporate taxes. This article offers suggestions to enhance domestic revenue mobilization strategies by looking at the opportunities available in some of the

government's major tax instruments then discusses government efforts to support fiscal consolidation.

OVERVIEW OF FIJI'S DOMESTIC REVENUE COMPONENTS

Fiji had higher tax revenue than most of its peers and comparable countries before 2019 but declined due to the impact of the pandemic on the economy and tax cuts implemented to encourage quick economic recovery (Figure 10). From 2010 to 2019, Fiji's average tax-to-GDP ratio was 23.0%, higher than in Asia and the Pacific (19.0%) but lower than the average of 33.0% for the OECD member countries.

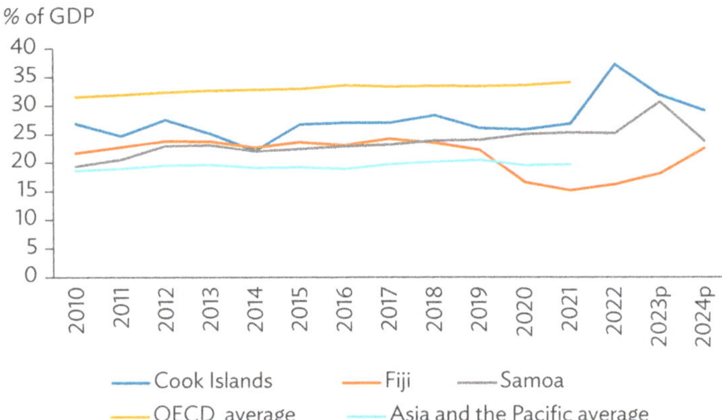

Figure 10: Cross-Country Tax Revenue Comparisons

GDP = gross domestic product, OECD = Organisation for Economic Co-operation and Development, p = projection.

Note: The fiscal year of the Government of Fiji ends on 31 July (starting 2016) and 30 June for the Government of the Cook Islands and the Government of Samoa.

Sources: ADB. Asian Development Outlook database (accessed 17 November 2023) and Organisation for Economic Co-operation and Development. 2023. *Revenue Statistics in Asia and the Pacific 2023*. Paris.

Fiji had to take some tough revenue measures to avert the declining tax revenue-to-GDP ratio trend. The government raised the VAT rate to 15.0% (from 9.0% and 12.5% for some items) in its recent FY2024 budget which is expected to increase VAT revenues by 50%. Other measures include increasing the corporate tax rate from 20% to 25% while departure tax for tourists will be increased gradually. The success of these revenue measures depends on a sustainable economic recovery path.

The primary contributors to government revenue are VAT, income tax (personal and corporate), and customs duties (Figure 11). Together, they make up more than 70.0% of total revenue.

VAT accounts for about 40.0% of total government revenue. It was first introduced in Fiji in 1992 with a single rate of 10.0% for all goods and services. From 2000 to 2015, the government removed VAT on basic food items and prescription medicines while the VAT rate for the rest was raised initially to 12.5% and then to 15.0% during this period. From 2016 to 2022, the government reduced the VAT rate to 9.0%. Starting in April 2022, a 3-tiered VAT system was used where basic food items were zero-rated, 15.0% was applied to luxury and tourism-related goods and services, and all other goods and services were charged a 9.0% rate. In its FY2024 budget, the government has reverted to a 2-tiered system with the VAT rate raised to 15.0% for most goods but kept the exemption for basic food items and prescribed medicines.

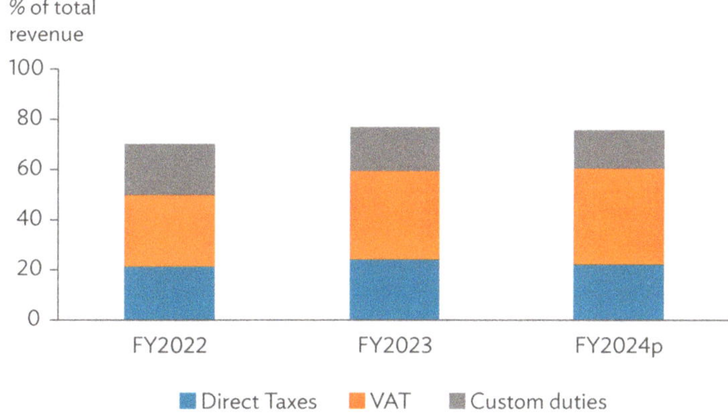

Figure 11: Contribution of Domestic Revenue to Fiji's Overall Government Revenue

FY = fiscal year, p = projection, VAT = value-added tax.
Note: The fiscal year of the Government of Fiji ends on 31 July.
Source: Government of Fiji. *Budget Supplement FY2023–2024*. Suva.

As a percentage of GDP, Fiji collected more VAT than the Asia and Pacific average from 2010 to 2020 and more than the OECD average from 2010 to 2015 (Figure 12). VAT revenue declined in 2016 but subsequently remained stable until the pandemic. Meanwhile, revenue from income, profits, and capital gains taxes (also as a share of GDP) remains below the Asia and Pacific average—and well below the OECD average—for most of 2010–2020.

Before 2001, the corporate income tax rate was at 35.0% for non-residents. To encourage companies to list on the South Pacific Stock Exchange, a 10.0% rate was introduced in 2014 but the take-up has been slow, creating doubts about whether the economic benefits gained from it outweigh the revenue loss. Meanwhile, dividends for shareholders of listed companies have been exempted from tax since 2000. Introducing a tax on dividends could provide another source of revenue for the government.

About 87.0% of Fiji's eligible taxpayers do not pay personal income tax as they earn below the income threshold of F$30,000 (Government of Fiji 2023a). This includes 88.0% of salaried employees, 81.0% of sole traders, and 61.0% of partnerships. While this may offer another potential revenue source in future, the timing, overall economic impact and equity consideration must be carefully evaluated before such an action can be pursued.

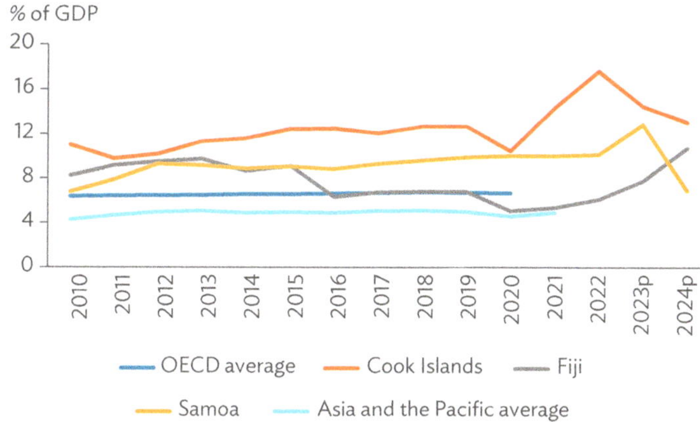

Figure 12: Cross-Country Value-Added Tax Collection Performance

GDP = gross domestic product, OECD = Organisation for Economic Co-operation and Development, p = projection.
Note: The fiscal year of the Government of Fiji ends on 31 July (starting 2016) and 30 June for the Government of Samoa.
Sources: ADB. Asian Development Outlook database (accessed 17 November 2023) and Organisation for Economic Co-operation and Development. 2023. *Revenue Statistics in Asia and the Pacific 2023*. Paris.

Customs duties are Fiji's third main contributor to total government revenues. As a share of GDP, Fiji collects more revenue from this source compared to the OECD and averages in Asia and the Pacific, but this is likely due to Fiji's high dependence on imported commodities as a small developing economy in the Pacific.

The IMF estimates that the reduction in taxes, tariffs, and excises in the FY2021 and FY2022 budgets may have caused a loss in government revenue equivalent to 5.0% of GDP (IMF 2021). The IMF proposed a roadmap for fiscal adjustment which includes simplifying personal income tax, increasing the VAT and departure tax, adjusting excise duties, reducing film tax rebates, and removing export incentives. The IMF estimates that its roadmap would generate an increase in government revenue equivalent to about 2.0% of GDP per year in the first 2 years and 0.3% of GDP per year in the following 2 years. In response, the government implemented similar forms of policy changes in the FY2024 budget which, together with the recovery in tax base, is expected to increase revenues by about 38.0% compared to the previous fiscal year.

EFFORTS TO REFORM TAXES

Several reforms have been put in place by the Fiji Revenue and Customs Service. These include the move toward a single broad-based VAT rate to streamline lodgments of returns, the establishment of new tax audit units for large taxpayers, the creation of a support center for small and medium-sized enterprises, and launch of a new compliance improvement strategy to encourage voluntary compliance and build user confidence in the tax systems. The Fiji Revenue and Customs Service also launched a VAT guide to increase awareness and minimize revenue leakage through improved compliance. The March 2023 rollout of the new tax information system facilitates filing by enabling taxpayers to lodge returns (such as corporate and personal income tax returns) online.

OPPORTUNITIES AND NEXT STEPS

A comprehensive review of revenue policies is essential for Fiji to enhance its domestic revenue mobilization strategies and enable financing of future development needs. Adopting a medium-term revenue strategy may be needed to anchor the government's fiscal goals. The pandemic has shown the importance of increased digitalization in essential tax administration functions, and this must be complemented with sound data analytics to accomplish meaningful and lasting improvements in tax administration. It is also vital to find the right balance between revenue collection and encouraging private sector growth. Numerous administrative requirements discourage potential investment and weaken the business environment.

Tax exemptions may also need to be carefully reviewed. To start with, it may be worthwhile to review whether past exemptions aimed at incentivizing investment have met their intended purposes. Anecdotal evidence suggests that in most cases tax exemptions result in net revenue loss because the number of firms availing the exemption is not enough to generate the level of investment that can make up for the lost revenue. It also complicates the tax system for investors and encourages rent-seeking behavior, which can adversely affect investor confidence.

With VAT contributing 40.0% of the government's revenue, it is essential to maintain the system's efficiency to boost collection and reduce noncompliance and revenue loss.

The pandemic has led to higher debt levels in many small island developing states—including Fiji—due to increased spending on health and economic measures amid reduced government revenues. As countries phase out fiscal stimulus measures, returning to pre-pandemic spending levels is not going to be easy. Further, the infrastructure investment backlog and increasing need for climate change adaptation and mitigation require notable capital investment. In recognition of these challenges, it is reassuring to see governments, such as Fiji's, putting in place concrete measures to begin the journey toward generating a sustainable level of tax revenues that can meet the country's development needs.

References

Asian Development Bank. 2020. *A Comparative Analysis of Tax Administration in Asia and the Pacific: 2020 Edition.* Manila.

Government of Fiji, 2023 Fiji Fiscal Review Committee. 2023a. *Report of the Committee.* Suva.

Government of Fiji, Ministry of Finance, Strategic Planning, National Development and Statistics. 2023b. *Medium Term Fiscal Strategy 2024-2026.* Parliamentary Paper No. 7 of 2023. Suva.

Government of Fiji, Ministry of Finance, Strategic Planning, National Development and Statistics. 2023c. *Budget Supplement 2023-2024.* Suva.

International Monetary Fund (IMF). 2021. Republic of Fiji 2021 Article IV Consultation. *IMF Country Report.* No. 21/257. Washington, DC.

IMF. 2023. *IMF Staff Completes 2023 Article IV Mission to Fiji. Press Release.* No. 23/86. 21 March.

M. Sy et al. 2022. Funding the Future: Tax Revenue Mobilization in the Pacific Island Countries. *Departmental Paper No. 2022/015.* Washington, DC: IMF.

Organisation for Economic Co-operation and Development. 2023. *Revenue Statistics in Asia and the Pacific 2023.* Paris.

World Bank. 2023. *Fiji Public Expenditure Review.* Washington, DC.

Strengthening domestic resource mobilization in Kiribati and Tuvalu

Lead authors: Lily-Anne Homasi, Isoa Wainiqolo, and Noel Del Castillo

Improving revenue collection through tax policy and administration reforms is critical for building resilience in Kiribati and Tuvalu. In 2022, tax receipts accounted for 17.6% of GDP in Kiribati and 12.1% of GDP in Tuvalu, both below the 19.8% subregional average for the Pacific. For years, these atoll nations have depended on volatile revenue sources—fishing license fees and budget support grants from development partners accounted for over 80.0% of GDP in 2022 in Kiribati and over 55.0% of GDP in Tuvalu—to finance their development priorities. In 2019, fishing license revenues alone averaged 83.5% of GDP in Kiribati and 49.0% of GDP in Tuvalu. Given the uncertainty of these revenue sources, challenges associated with low capacity and limited digitalization of tax services, and the need to strengthen Kiribati and Tuvalu domestic revenue streams, it is vital to rethink tax policy and tax administration initiatives to support fiscal sustainability. This article will explore the challenges—and progress thus far—in enhancing tax compliance and efficiency to achieve fiscal self-sufficiency in these atoll nations.

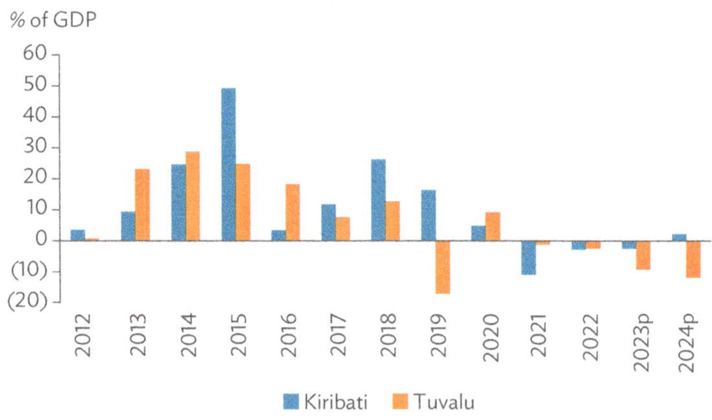

Figure 13: Fiscal Balance of Kiribati and Tuvalu

( ) = negative, GDP = gross domestic product, p = projection.
Sources: ADB. 2023. *Asian Development Outlook September 2023.* Manila; Government of Kiribati. *Recurrent Budget.* Tarawa (11 years: 2012–2022); and Government of Tuvalu. National Budget. Funafuti. (11 years: 2012–2022).

KIRIBATI

Kiribati had fiscal surpluses every year from 2012 to 2020. However, it recorded a deficit equivalent to 11.0% of GDP in 2021 amid muted revenues and soaring spending, which jumped 16.9% in 2021, to support social protection initiatives during the COVID-19 pandemic. By 2022, the fiscal position had improved but continued to remain in deficit. This deficit is expected to persist in 2023 as forecasts indicate lower government revenues amid sustained higher expenditure (Figure 13).

The country relies on three major revenue sources: fishing licenses—which average almost three-quarters of total revenue—taxes, and grants from development partners. The Asian Development Outlook September 2023 reported that Kiribati's fishing license revenue is expected to decline in 2023 due to changing weather patterns which will affect fish catches (ADB 2023). The expected weaker performance of this sector could have a significant adverse impact on the overall fiscal position. The country's high reliance on a volatile revenue source puts impetus on the need to increase internal revenue sources to improve the stability of the country's finances (Figure 14).

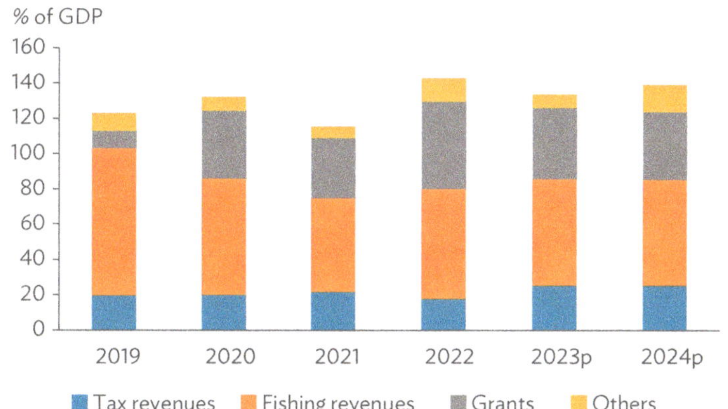

Figure 14: Kiribati Revenue Composition

GDP = gross domestic product, p = projection.

Note: Fishing revenues include fishing license fees, transshipment fees, and other fisheries-related revenue.

Sources: ADB. Asian Development Outlook database (accessed 13 November 2023); Government of Kiribati. *Recurrent Budget*. Tarawa. (5 years: 2019–2023).

In 2022, tax revenue accounted for 17.6% of GDP, 2.2 percentage points below the 19.8% regional average for Asia and the Pacific. Inadequate laws, capacity constraints, and limited tools—including an outdated revenue management system to administer tax—are some of the issues faced by the Government of Kiribati taxation division, leading to low compliance and resulting in foregone revenues. Sparse government tax audits of firms weaken its ability to enforce tax obligations and collect revenue.

To address these issues and to broaden Kiribati's tax base, Parliament passed an amendment to the 1990 Income Tax Act in September 2023 to improve tax administration and compliance. The amended Act includes provisions for setting up a simplified tax regime for small businesses, anti-avoidance rules, tax accounting rules, and clearer tax procedural rules. It also introduces new tax policy measures to expand the tax base, including a new tax regime for seabed mining operations and an international transportation income tax on nonresidents operating a ship or aircraft. This could improve revenue collection as well as strengthen tax administration and compliance to plug tax leakage brought about by weak monitoring. Corporate tax revenue averaged only 3.8% of total revenue from 2016 to 2020.

The government has also embarked on structural reforms to improve oversight and management of 18 state-owned enterprises (SOEs) in Kiribati. Through the reforms, over 60% of SOEs have complied in submitting their statements of intent and financial statements which are crucial in providing essential information to the taxation division to assess and collect income tax revenue that could be gained to support public services.

The government can consider bolstering its tax audit capacity as the next priority in its efforts to increase tax compliance. Capacity constraints continue to persist. A technical assistance support to restructure the Kiribati Tax Division to add and train more staff in this area will elevate the timeliness and quality of tax audit of the division and inform debt collection efforts to boost revenues.

TUVALU

Similar to Kiribati, Tuvalu has mostly posted fiscal surpluses from 2012 to 2020. The pandemic significantly altered Tuvalu's fiscal position (Figure 13). The government mobilization of its pandemic response package under a weak revenue environment resulted in fiscal deficits equivalent to 1.3% of GDP in 2021 and 2.5% of GDP in 2022. The deficit is expected to widen in 2023 to 9.2% of GDP and 11.9% of GDP in 2024 as the government resumes and ramps up its infrastructure spending. With committed grants being included as revenue, government may have to source additional grants or cut back on its budget to meet its financing gap.

As a small island economy with an exclusive economic zone of more than 750,000 square kilometers, Tuvalu's primary source of revenue comes from fishing licenses (Figure 15). Tax revenues, on average, only account for one-seventh of the country's total revenue. Meanwhile, grants from development partners, accounting for one-fifth of the total revenue, have a larger share than taxes in the government's finances. The IMF has estimated that during 2010–2021, Tuvalu's tax revenue accounted for less than one-fifth of its GDP (IMF 2023). Mobilizing domestic revenues would not only help Tuvalu achieve fiscal consolidation but will also broaden its revenue sources and increase and stabilize flows.

The IMF (2023)—in its Article IV report—suggested specific strategies for mobilizing domestic revenues. These include raising the VAT statutory rate in line with country peers; pushing for higher tax compliance and increasing the staff of the tax department; enhancing corporate income tax efficiency through an updated taxpayer registry, the rollout of e-payment and filing mechanisms, tax awareness activities and enforcement of timely filing, among others;

a targeted reversal of tax exemptions; and the enforcement of timely corporate reporting and auditing of SOE financial statements.

Broadening the tax base and improving tax compliance—particularly from businesses—are key domestic revenue mobilization strategies for Tuvalu. The IMF (2021) reported that only 2 of 21 registered large taxpayers currently pay corporate tax. From 2016 to 2019, corporate tax averaged only 1.9% of all revenue in Tuvalu. The government can consider prioritizing on updating its taxpayer registry to ensure that all businesses in the country are accounted for. Digitization of the documents and the eventual automation of the registration process can create a more efficient and reliable tax registration system. Meanwhile, capacity-building and boosting staff resources will support tax audits, which are integral to the functioning and credibility of tax administration.

Figure 15: Tuvalu Revenue Composition

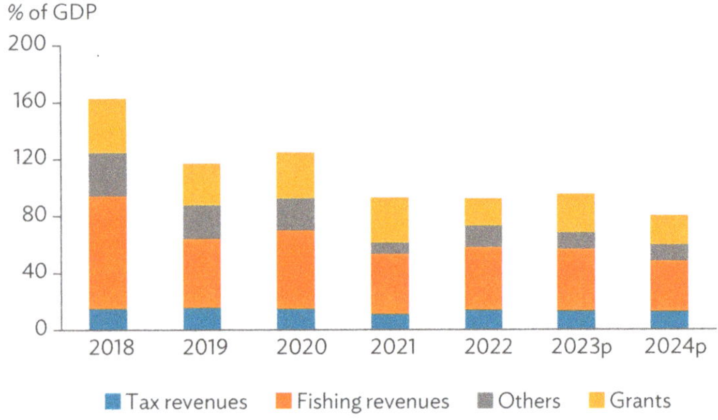

GDP = gross domestic product, p = projection.
Sources: ADB. Asian Development Outlook database (accessed 13 November 2023); Government of Tuvalu. *National Budget*. Funafuti. (11 years: 2012–2022).

The Government of Tuvalu understands the importance of ensuring fiscal sustainability and has emphasized plans to increase tax compliance. Given the recent implementation of the sin tax law, increasing compliance is the government's preferred strategy as it does not see scope for measures that could increase the burden for consumers. With most goods—and especially almost all food items—imported, Tuvaluans are already confronted with global inflation pressures and import duties.

LOOKING AHEAD

Kiribati and Tuvalu both recognize the limitations of tax administration and have an appetite to increase tax revenues in several ways:

(i)   Better tax administration of existing tax types—particularly income tax and value-added tax—through timely assessments of tax returns. Tax audits and debt management should improve tax collection.

(ii)   Development of revenue management strategies that will—among others—determine the staff requirements to achieve revenue targets, and technological improvements to support tax administration such as digitization of tax records.

(iii)   Strengthening the capacity of tax administrators and personnel in assessing filed taxes; conducting tax audits; and conducting analysis to inform pipeline work programs through targeted on-the-job training, group training, and more formal training.

(iv)   Six monthly and/or annual reviews of the performance of various sections within tax departments are critical to inform future work programming exercises.

These activities are all critical but need government backing through budgetary support and additional officers in technical fields such as auditing. Development partner support could supplement these efforts through technical and advisory services. Such services would need to consider the operating context and capacity constraints in these atoll nations.

References

Asian Development Bank (ADB). Asian Development Outlook Database for Kiribati (accessed 13 November 2023).

ADB. Asian Development Outlook Database for Tuvalu (accessed 13 November 2023).

ADB. 2023. *Asian Development Outlook September 2023*. Manila.

International Monetary Fund (IMF). 2023. *Kiribati: 2023 Article IV Consultation—Press Release and Staff Report*. Washington, DC.

IMF. 2023. *Tuvalu: 2023 Article IV Consultation—Press Release; Staff Report; and Statement by the Executive Director for Tuvalu*. Washington, DC.

Organisation for Economic Co-operation and Development. 2023. *Revenue Statistics in Asia and the Pacific 2023: Strengthening Property Taxation in Asia*. Paris.

M. Sy et al. 2022. Funding the Future: Tax Revenue Mobilization in the PICs. *Departmental Paper No. 2022/015*. Washington, DC: IMF.

Tax reform in Nauru, Solomon Islands, and Vanuatu: Challenges and opportunities

Lead authors: Katherine Passmore and Prince Cruz

The 2023 fiscal situations in Nauru, Solomon Islands, and Vanuatu are significantly worse than their pre-pandemic positions. All three economies face declines in key sources of revenue, highlighting a great need for strengthened domestic resource mobilization. While the three countries have long reform agendas, this article focuses on recent initiatives and opportunities for tax reform to enhance sustainable revenue sources and improve fiscal self-reliance.

THE URGENT NEED FOR TAX REFORM

In Nauru, revenue related to the Regional Processing Centre (RPC) rose from 39.5% of domestic revenues in FY2015 (ended on 30 June) to an average of 64.7% during FY2020–FY2022. As the RPC entered enduring capability mode in July 2023, revenues related to its operations including personal and company taxes fell.[1] The fiscal surplus fell to 14.3% of GDP in FY2023 from an average of 23.3% during FY2020–FY2022 (Figure 16). Although funding for the RPC has been agreed upon until FY2026, there is no guarantee of funding beyond then.

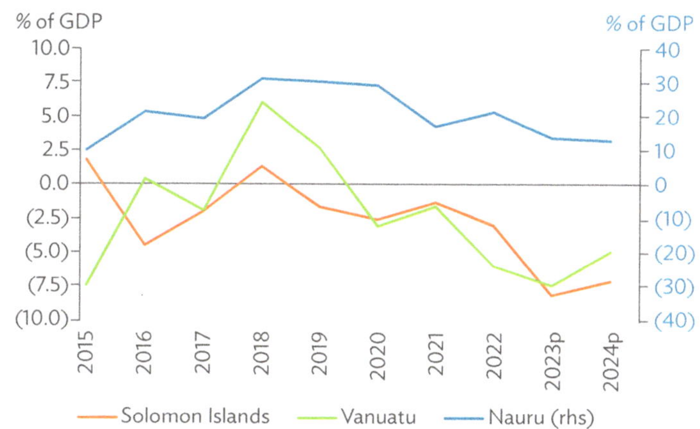

Figure 16: Fiscal Balances of Nauru, Solomon Islands, and Vanuatu

( ) = negative, GDP = gross domestic product, p = projection, rhs = right-hand scale.

Note: The fiscal year of the Government of Nauru ends on 30 June.

Sources: ADB estimates using budget documents from the Central Bank of Solomon Islands. *Quarterly Review*. Honiara (8 years: 2015–2022); Government of Nauru, Ministry of Finance. *Budget Paper No 1*. Yaren (8 years: FY2016–FY2023); Government of Vanuatu, Ministry of Finance and Economic Management. Budget. Port Vila (8 years: 2015–2022).

In Solomon Islands, the fiscal situation was tight even before the pandemic with a deficit averaging 0.9% of GDP from 2015 to 2019. Pandemic-related restrictions and the government's move toward sustainable logging output led to a rapid decline in log output contributing to an economic contraction from 2020 to 2022. Although the value of export duties on logs has never exceeded 20.0% of government revenues, the outsized impact of logging on the economy indicates that revenues are expected to decline in the future as log output continues to fall. The fiscal deficit is projected to widen to 7.5% of GDP in 2023–2024 from an average of 2.1% during 2020–2022 (Table 1).

In Vanuatu, the Honorary Citizenship Programs (HCPs), under which honorary passports are offered in exchange for contributions to the program, were revised in 2015 to help finance the reconstruction from Cyclone Pam. As the European Union and the United Kingdom have restricted visa-free access to Vanuatu passport holders, the HCPs have lost their main pull. This contributed to the fiscal balance turning from a surplus of 0.1% of GDP during 2015–2019 to a deficit of 3.4% during 2020–2022. The deficit is projected to deteriorate further to 6.1% of GDP during 2023–2024.

Without major reform, the revenue decline in all three countries will affect debt sustainability and public service delivery, including health, education, and social protection. Investment in education and training is critical as the need for skilled workers intensifies and labor mobility schemes impact worker availability. There is also a need to address the massive infrastructure needs caused by years of underinvestment and damage from natural hazards.[2]

In terms of public debt levels, Solomon Islands has kept its debt-to-GDP ratio relatively low since the 1990s. However, debt is projected to rapidly increase as projects that stalled due to the pandemic are implemented. In Vanuatu, debt accumulated for reconstruction following Cyclone Pam in 2015 and Cyclone Harold in 2020 has not been fully paid off, and additional spending is

Table 1: Fiscal Balance and Tax Reform in Nauru, Solomon Islands, and Vanuatu

	Nauru	Solomon Islands	Vanuatu
Major revenue issue	Decline of Regional Processing Centre revenues	Decline in logging related revenues	Decline in Honorary Citizenship Programs revenue
Average fiscal balance (% of GDP)			
2015–2019	23.2	(0.9)	0.1
2020–2022	23.3	(2.1)	(3.4)
2023–2024	13.9	(7.5)	(6.1)
Recent tax reform	Introduction of income taxes and tax administration improvements (2014–2016)	Adjusted personal income tax threshold (2019) Tax Administration Act (2022)	Increase in VAT rate from 12.5% to 15.0% (2018)
Tax reform opportunities	Review income tax regime; introduce VAT	Shift to VAT (underway)	Introduce personal and corporate income taxes

( ) = negative, GDP = gross domestic product, VAT = value-added tax.

Note: The fiscal year of the Government of Nauru ends on 30 June.

Source: Authors' compilation.

needed for reconstruction after the March and October 2023 cyclones. In Nauru, external debt has been significantly reduced, but the government is still paying off domestic debt assumed after the economic collapse in the 1990s.

NAURU

Since 2014, Nauru has undergone significant tax reform, which has improved revenue collection and led to an increase of over 30% in Nauru's tax-to-GDP ratio from FY2014 to FY2020.[3] The major reforms have been the introduction of income tax in 2014 through the *Employment and Services Tax Act*, and a business profits tax in 2016. Due to local pushback to the reform, the personal income tax-free threshold is high at A$110,880 for Nauru citizens, well above the initially proposed threshold of A$20,400. For reference, GDP per capita in 2016 was A$8,641.

The result is a very narrow tax base, as only a small portion of potential taxpayers is captured. Non-residents are subject to a lower threshold. Once the threshold is met, there is a flat tax rate of 20%, unless income is derived from the RPC in which case the rate is 30%.[4] Despite the narrow base, this tax generated A$12.6 million in its first full fiscal year of implementation in FY2016.[5] The business profits tax also has a narrow base, with a tax-free threshold for Nauru citizens of A$250,000. The tax rate ranges from 20% to 25%, determined by turnover and residency status. In FY2022, the business profits tax generated A$40 million in revenue, representing 14% of total government revenue.

In support of these reforms, the government has also improved tax administration through the introduction of the Revenue Administration Act in 2014, accompanied by taxpayer education and registration support to promote compliance. From 2018 to 2020, nearly 100% of business taxpayers reportedly filed on time and electronically.[6] Implementation of the ASYCUDA is also expected to improve compliance and boost customs revenue.

Despite these gains, after nearly 10 years of implementation, projected revenue from the personal and corporate income tax is expected to decline by approximately 85% in FY2024 from its peak in FY2021 due to the winding down of the RPC.[7] Revenue from these taxes is expected to decline from 27% of total revenue in FY2021 to just 4% in FY2024 (Figure 17). To counter this lost revenue, the government should consider further tax reform to enable domestic resource mobilization.

As part of a broader tax reform strategy that is less reliant on external sources, broadens the tax base, and generates more consistent revenue, key areas for policymaker attention include income and consumption taxes, and tax administration. In terms of income taxes, the government may consider gradually lowering the tax-free threshold for income taxes to broaden the tax base over the medium to long term. Meanwhile, Nauru is one of few Pacific economies yet to implement a broad consumption tax such as VAT. While the prospect of increased prices for consumers is politically unpopular, it is estimated that the introduction of VAT could generate up to $8.8 million per year, or 6.6% of GDP.[8] Regional lessons on recent

VAT implementation should be considered, including from very small island economies such as the Cook Islands, Kiribati, and Niue.[9] As for tax administration, the Nauru Revenue Office is receiving support for an assessment of its tax administration and options for digitalization, which have the potential to improve compliance. Such efforts should continue as part of a staged medium-term tax strategy.

Figure 17: Nauru Domestic Revenue

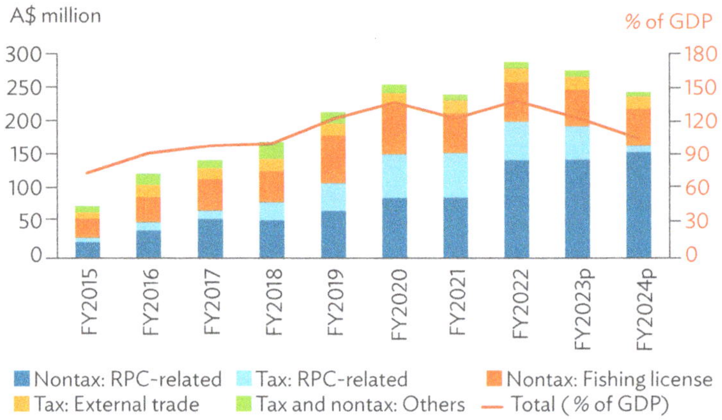

A$ = Australian dollar, FY = fiscal year, GDP = gross domestic product, p = projection, RPC = Regional Processing Centre.

Note: The fiscal year of the Government of Nauru ends on 30 June.

Sources: ADB estimates; Government of Nauru, Ministry of Finance. *Budget Paper No 1*. Yaren (8 years: FY2016–FY2023).

SOLOMON ISLANDS

In the face of a deteriorating fiscal position, the Government of Solomon Islands has embarked on extensive tax reform. Tax revenue accounts for more than 85% of domestic revenue, but projected reductions in logging activity are expected to significantly impact collections, creating a pressing need for reform (Figure 18).

A 2017 government review concluded that the prevailing tax structure—largely unchanged since independence in 1978—impedes economic growth. The tax regime was described as "outdated, inefficient, complex, expensive to administer, and anti-competitive".[10] A tax reform agenda has since been developed based on the principles of fairness, simplicity, efficiency, competitiveness, and accountability. The initial components of the reform are a review of consumption taxes—taxes on the purchase of goods and services—and tax administration.

Consumption taxes are generally considered a reliable government revenue source, but the consumption tax framework in Solomon Islands is cumbersome and a constraint to economic growth, consisting of a variety of taxes such as goods tax, sales tax, an accommodation levy, and stamp duty. Taxes on goods and services have accounted for an average of 27% of tax revenue from 2015 to 2022. In addition to increasing the cost of doing business and costs to consumers, these taxes are unfairly applied due to compliance issues and discretionary exemptions and therefore apply to a narrow base. They also hamper the development of export markets due to a lack of competitiveness, as Solomon Islander exporters pay indirect tax on business inputs, competing with exporters from other countries who do not necessarily pay such taxes.

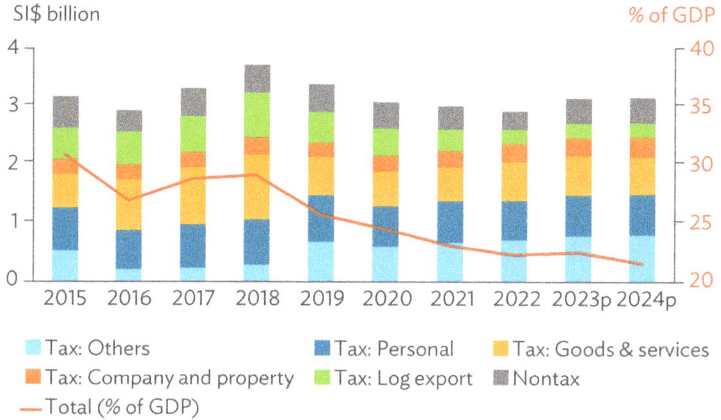

Figure 18: Solomon Islands Domestic Revenue

GDP = gross domestic product, p = projection, SI$ = Solomon Islands dollar.
Sources: ADB estimates; Central Bank of Solomon Islands. *Quarterly Review*. Honiara (8 years: 2015–2022).

After extensive consultation, a VAT bill has been tabled in Parliament and is expected to be enacted by 2025. The proposed VAT rate is 15%, with a registration threshold of SI$2 million. Upon enactment of the VAT, various taxes on goods and services will be repealed. Fiscal modeling indicates an initial neutral impact on revenue, but a 5% gain in overall tax revenue within 2 years of implementation due to improved efficiency and growth in the tax base.[11] The fairer, streamlined, broad-based consumption tax is expected to improve revenue generation, reduce compliance costs for taxpayers, and promote competitiveness.

The government has also embarked on extensive reforms to improve tax administration and the capacity of tax authorities, including through the *Tax Administration Act 2022*, which simplifies administration procedures and penalties. The inland revenue division is undergoing restructuring, business process improvement, capability enhancements, and deployment of a new tax administration system. These reforms are expected to improve efficiency and compliance, boost revenue, and reduce administration costs. The IMF has found that such reforms can increase the tax-to-GDP ratio by up to 9%.[12] Current estimates indicate that the value of revenue foregone due to non-compliance is significant. For example, the introduction of a large taxpayer office—dedicated to supporting compliance of the largest 50 taxpayers, based on turnover—reportedly led to a 50% reduction in the tax debt in the first 12 months of operation. The next stage of reform is a comprehensive income tax review.[13]

While the government has taken great strides in reforming the tax regime, it will take time for the benefits to be realized. Due to the long-term nature of these reforms, sustained political will—along with the education of taxpayers and tax authorities—will be critical

to successful implementation. A transparent and fairly applied tax system will improve the confidence of the private sector and investors. If implemented with strengthened public expenditure measures, compliance in the medium to long term is likely to improve and lead to even greater gains, as the quality of government expenditure and taxpayer compliance are mutually reinforcing.

VANUATU

After Cyclone Pam struck Vanuatu in 2015, the government reorganized its HCPs to raise funds for reconstruction and rehabilitation.[14] From Vt3.6 billion (4.2% of GDP) in 2016, HCP revenues rose rapidly peaking at Vt14.4 billion (13.7% of GDP) in 2020 (Figure 19). With pandemic-related restrictions on international travel, HCP revenues dipped in 2021 but remained the biggest contributor to total revenues, outpacing VAT since 2018. The decline accelerated in 2022 with HCP revenues plunging 34% to Vt8.5 billion (7.5% of GDP).

Figure 19: Vanuatu Domestic Revenue

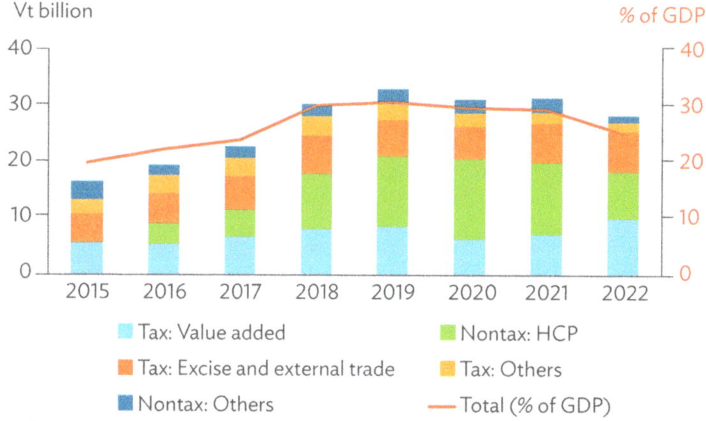

HCP = honorary citizenship program, GDP = gross domestic product, Vt = vatu.
Sources: ADB estimates; Government of Vanuatu, Ministry of Finance and Economic Management. *Budget*. Port Vila (8 years: 2015–2022). Port Vila.

As HCP provides foreign investors with secondary passports, its main draw is linked to the strength of the Vanuatu passport for visa-free international travel. In March 2022, the Council of the European Union implemented a partial suspension of its visa waiver program with Vanuatu for passports issued after 2016. Citing several concerns, the European Union announced in November 2022 the full suspension of the visa waiver program for all Vanuatu passport holders by February 2023. After an urgent appeal by the government, the full suspension was delayed until August 2024, to give the authorities more time to tighten HCP regulations. In July 2023, the United Kingdom also terminated its visa waiver for Vanuatu passport holders.

As HCP revenues are projected to continue declining, the IMF has identified an urgent need for "Revenue mobilization policies, including updating and completing the proposed 2017 tax reforms, which envisioned the introduction of corporate and personal income taxes."[15] These reforms originated from the government-led Vanuatu Revenue Review, launched in 2016, which sought to broaden the revenue base; reduce the cost of doing business; lower the cost of living and cost of capital to support investment and economic growth; and modernize tax administration for fair, transparent, and effective revenue collection.[16] The review focused on the introduction of corporate and personal income taxes and included public consultations regarding the reforms.

The proposed corporate income tax rate was 17% for most companies, while the proposed personal income tax rate was 10% for income between Vt750,001 and Vt3.5 million, and 17% for income above Vt3.5 million. For reference, the average GDP per capita in 2016 was Vt310,898, while the minimum annual wage was around Vt360,000.

The proposed personal and corporate income tax was projected to generate Vt4.2 billion (4.6% of GDP) in 2018, rising to Vt7.4 billion (5.2% of GDP) in 2026 (Figure 20). The additional revenues—expected to well outpace several existing fees and taxes—would allow the government to repeal rent tax, business license fees, and turnover tax, and reduce import duties, lowering the cost of doing business. Further, the additional revenues were planned to finance free education up to Year 10, increase health expenditure, provide more funds for provinces and councils, and contribute to a fiscal responsibility or development fund.

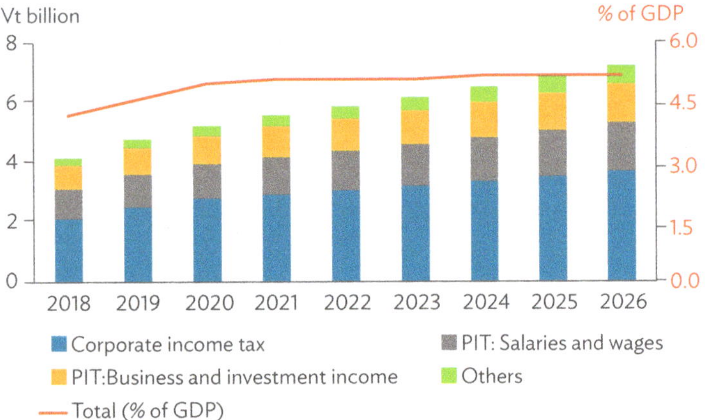

Figure 20: Projected Additional Revenues from New Taxes in Vanuatu

GDP = gross domestic product, PIT = personal income tax, Vt = vatu.

Source: Government of Vanuatu. 2017. *Vanuatu Revenue Review: Final Report on the Case for Revenue Reform and Modernisation*. Port Vila.

Some business groups opposed the introduction of income taxes and suggested that the VAT rate and other fees and charges should be raised instead. The review concluded that the proposed increase in VAT did not meet the principles of good revenue systems in terms of the fairness principle. However, the 2017 proposal to introduce income taxes stalled, and in 2018, the government instead raised the VAT rate from 12.5% to 15.0%. VAT collections rose 19.4% from Vt6.9 billion (7.3% of GDP) in 2017 to Vt8.2 billion (8.2% of GDP) in 2018. With pandemic-related restrictions, economic activity contracted in 2020, reducing VAT collections to Vt6.5 billion (6.2% of GDP) before gradually recovering to Vt10.1 billion (9.0% of GDP) in 2022.

COMMON CHALLENGES TO TAX REFORM

Impacts on economic growth and inflation. Consumption taxes inevitably contribute to higher prices and may negatively impact economic activity. In the high inflation environments that these three developing member countries face in 2023, there may be little appetite for such tax increases (Figure 21).[17] In fact, Nauru, Solomon Islands, and Vanuatu have responded to cost-of-living pressures by reducing import duties.[18]

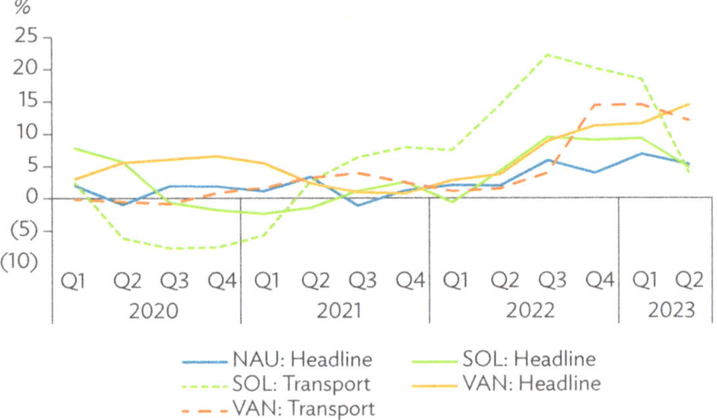

Figure 21: Headline and Transport Inflation in Nauru, Solomon Islands, and Vanuatu

NAU = Nauru, Q = quarter, SOL = Solomon Islands, VAN = Vanuatu.

Sources: Central Bank of Solomon Islands. 2023. *Quarterly Review June 2023*. Honiara; Government of Nauru, Ministry of Finance. 2023. *Budget Paper No 1*. Yaren; Government of Vanuatu, Bureau of Statistics. *Statistics Update: Consumer Price Index June Quarter 2023 Highlights*. Port Vila (September).

Policymakers should bear in mind that the inflationary impacts of new taxes are often temporary, while the benefits such as fiscal stability and improved public service delivery are long term. In Vanuatu for example, there were fears that inflation would accelerate in 2018 with the higher VAT rate, resulting in consumers bringing forward purchases in anticipation of the higher rate.[19] Inflation accelerated to 3.6% in the third quarter of 2017 from an average of 0.8% in 2016 but decelerated to 1.8% by the third quarter of 2018.

Narrow economic bases. With economic growth driven mainly by the government and one major industry or sector (the RPC for Nauru, logging for Solomon Islands, and tourism for Vanuatu), the options for new taxes are limited. With the bulk of the population in subsistence agriculture in Solomon Islands and Vanuatu, collecting new or more taxes from this sector is difficult. This gives rise to a common pushback against tax reform: that a certain subset of wealthy taxpayers is already overtaxed.[20] One main goal of tax reform is to make the tax base as wide as possible to lower the tax rate imposed. The tax collected can be used to invest in human and physical capital that can widen the economic base in the medium-to long-term and support improved livelihoods, ensuring the benefits of tax reform are felt widely.

Political instability. With the long-term nature, complexity, and inherent unpopularity of tax reform, strong political will is needed to carry it through. If the ruling coalition or party has narrow control of the legislature or is in constant threat of a no-confidence motion, passage of reforms may be exceedingly difficult. Widespread awareness of the benefits of tax reform can help spur broad-based support from the community and the private sector. The *Asian Development Outlook* in 2022 highlighted that "Tax reform to boost revenue is politically challenging, but global experience shows that strong leadership can inspire buy-in and bring success."[21]

CONCLUSION

Nauru, Solomon Islands, and Vanuatu all face challenging fiscal situations as key sources of revenue decline. Domestic resource mobilization—in particular tax reform—should be considered as part of a holistic revenue strategy to maintain long-term fiscal stability. While Nauru and Solomon Islands have committed to ambitious reforms, more modest reforms have been seen in Vanuatu.

Although tax reform is challenging, examples from the region provide lessons and demonstrate positive impacts. Strong political will is essential due to the long-term nature of tax reform design and implementation, as is the need to consider vulnerable groups in the design.

The 2023 economic and political climates present a particularly challenging period for tax reform. However, forward-looking reforms that are well-considered and -designed—and implemented in conjunction with improved public expenditure measures—are expected to provide material benefit to citizens and support a path to fiscal self-reliance.

Endnotes

[1] "Enduring capability" reflects a memorandum of understanding between the Government of Australia and the Government of Nauru to maintain RPC capability. It is understood that new arrivals to the RPC in September and November 2023 have resulted in a low level of RPC activity.

[2] Asian Development Bank (ADB). 2017. Box 5.2: Infrastructure Investment Needs in the Pacific in *Meeting Asia's Infrastructure Needs*. Manila.

[3] The World Bank. 2023. *Raising Pasifika: Strengthening Government Finance to Enhance Human Capital in the Pacific.* Washington DC.

[4] Government of Nauru. 2014. *Employment and Services Tax Act 2014.* Yaren.

[5] ADB. 2017. *Nauru: Fiscal Sustainability Reform Program.* Manila.

[6] International Monetary Fund (IMF). *International Survey on Revenue Administration* (accessed 30 October 2023); and The World Bank. 2023. *Raising Pasifika: Strengthening Government*

[7] Finance to Enhance Human Capital in the Pacific. Washington DC. Government of Nauru. 2023. *2023–24 Budget: Budget Paper No 1.* Yaren.

[8] The World Bank. 2023. *Raising Pasifika: Strengthening Government Finance to Enhance Human Capital in the Pacific.* Washington DC.

[9] VAT was introduced in the Cook Islands in 1997, Niue in 2009, and Kiribati in 2014. See K. Murray, R. Oliver, and S. Wyatt. 2014. *Evaluation of taxation reform in the Pacific.* Report prepared for the New Zealand Ministry of Foreign Affairs and Trade.

[10] Government of Solomon Islands. 2017. *Solomon Islands: The Case for Tax Reform.* Honiara.

[11] The World Bank. 2022. *Solomon Islands Public Expenditure Review: Fiscal Reforms and the Path to Debt Sustainability.* Washington DC.

[12] IMF. 2023. *Building Tax Capacity in Developing Countries.* Washington DC.

[13] In 2019, the income tax threshold was adjusted from SI$15,080 to SI$30,080. The GDP per capita in 2019 was SI$16,028. The estimated foregone revenue from the adjustment was SI$83.4 million. National Parliament of Solomon Islands. 2019. *Report on the Income Tax (Amendment) Bill 2019.* Honiara.

[14] ADB. 2019. Managing unconventional revenue streams. Pacific Economic Monitor. Manila (December).

[15] IMF. 2023. Vanuatu 2023 Article IV Consultation—Press Release; Staff Report; and Statement by the Executive Director for Vanuatu. *IMF Country Report No. 23/115.* Washington DC.

[16] Government of Vanuatu. 2017. *Vanuatu Revenue Review: Final Report on the Case for Revenue Reform and Modernisation.* Port Vila.

[17] Inflation rates in the three Pacific developing member countries are at historical highs, mainly due to the lagged pass-through of high global commodity prices and—in Vanuatu—additional price pressures from the impact of the March cyclones on agriculture and domestic supply chains.

[18] In September 2023, the Government of Vanuatu reduced import duties on petroleum, rice, and chicken wings to reduce inflationary pressures. Pump prices of petroleum fell by 2.5% to 5.0% due to the reduction in duties. In June 2022, the Government of Solomon Islands reduced the import duty on fuel by 50.0% and exempted fuel from sales tax, which lowered retail prices by about 2.4%. From September to December 2022, the import duty on fuel was eliminated. In Nauru, the government cut import duties on petroleum in June 2022. While these import duty reductions somewhat relieved cost-of-living pressures, they led to foregone revenue for the government.

[19] ADB. 2018. *Asian Development Outlook 2018 Update: Maintaining Stability Amid Heightened Uncertainty.* Manila (September).

[20] J. Lakin. 2020. *The Politics of Tax Reform in Low- and Middle-income Countries: A Literature Review.* International Budget Partnership.

[21] ADB. 2022. *Asian Development Outlook 2022: Mobilizing Taxes for Development.* Manila.

Opportunities and constraints to domestic resource mobilization in Niue

Lead author: Isoa Wainiqolo

Niue is ADB's smallest developing member country by economic size. Domestic revenue was equivalent to 66.0% of total revenues in FY2019 (ended on 30 June) and the government projects this share to stabilize at around 70.0% in FY2023 and FY2024 through the recovery of tourism-related revenues. Given that tourism arrivals and related revenue can be volatile, the government will have to rely on other internal revenue sources—such as taxes—to sustain revenue levels. At the same time, any attempt to broaden the tax base must be carefully evaluated in consideration of Niue's small population. Likewise, vulnerability to climate change is likely to continue placing consistent pressures on its fiscal envelope. To sustain its no-debt strategy, it will need to step up its efforts on domestic revenue mobilization.

Domestic revenue was around 53.0% of GDP in FY2019 before the COVID-19 pandemic and has yet to fully recover in line with the tourism outlook. Niue's main revenue sources are recurrent budget support from the Government of New Zealand, income tax, customs duties, VAT, departure tax, and fishing license fees.

In the 2022 Census, Niue's population was 1,564. The country's dependency ratio of 94 dependents (children and retirees) for every 100 working-age persons is also much higher than the 72 dependents for the Cook Islands and the 79 dependents for Samoa (Table 2).

While a relatively low percentage of taxpayers hinders the development of volume-based tax collection measures, average Niuean households spend only 0.3% on taxes and fines as against the corporate tax rate of 30.0%, based on the 2015–2016 Household Income and Expenditure Survey. This potentially allows room to raise additional revenue from goods and services taxes such as VAT and customs duties.

Niue is also progressing on the international stage as it became a signatory to the OECD's Multilateral Convention on Mutual Administrative Assistance in Tax Matters in 2015, joining the efforts against offshore tax evasion and avoidance after signing.

There remain opportunities for generating additional revenue from better revenue administration measures. The 2020 Public Expenditure and Financial Accountability Performance Assessment for Niue highlighted that while some measures were in place to improve revenue administration, there was potential room for growth in the areas of revenue risk management, audit and investigation, and arrears monitoring. The government is working on a Niue Customs and Tax Administration Bill to address these gaps. Niue's tax administration and revenue management benefit from close coordination as both the Niue Taxation Office and Niue Customs are part of the Ministry of Finance. There may also be benefits from digitalizing tax systems (see page 34). Niue's small population may work in its favor with the advance of technology that can use data analytics to inform revenue collection strategies.

References

Government of Niue. 2018. *Niue 2015–2016 Household Income and Expenditure Survey*. Alofi.

Government of Niue. 2021. *Niue PEFA Performance Report 2020*. Alofi.

Government of Niue. 2023. *Budget Statement 2023-2024*. Alofi.

Government of Niue. 2023. *Niue Census of Population and Housing November 2022 Preliminary Report*. Alofi.

Table 2: Niue Resident Population, by Age Bracket

Life stage	2017		2022	
	Persons	% of total	Persons	% of total
Child (0–14)	447	28.1	409	26.2
Working age adult (15–59)	846	53.2	806	51.5
Retirement age (60+)	298	18.7	349	22.3
Total	1,591	100.0	1,564	100.0
Median age (years)	33		35	
Dependency ratio	88.1		94.0	

Source: Government of Niue. 2023. *Niue Census of Population and Housing November 2022 Preliminary Report*. Alofi.

Papua New Guinea's commitment to strengthening non-tax revenue administration and collection

Lead author: Darrell Freund

The collection and mobilization of non-tax revenue (NTR) in Papua New Guinea (PNG) achieved an important milestone in February 2018 when the Public Money Management Regulation Act (PMMR) came into effect. The act was an attempt by the government to implement policies for fees and charges that statutory bodies and agencies collect to fund their internal operations. Before the PMMR enactment, the NTR remittance to the Consolidated Revenue Fund was at the discretion of the bodies that collected the revenue. Following the effectiveness of the act, NTR increased to K2.9 billion in 2018 (22.0% higher than in 2017). Although in 2019, NTR declined to K2.3 billion, however, this was mainly due to reduced dividends from state-owned enterprises.

In May 2020, the PNG Supreme Court declared the PMMR unconstitutional and invalid after the Ombudsman Commission contested the law. The court found the act unconstitutional for eight reasons, including the restrictions it placed on filing judicial reviews for decisions rendered by the Strategic Budget Committee. The government established a committee to determine the amount of revenue that statutory bodies were permitted to retain. An important lesson learned from this invalidation of the PMMR was the need for a robust consultative process with stakeholders when drafting the next iteration of the PNG principal NTR regulation.

The invalidation of the PMMR and, later, the COVID-19 shock made it even more difficult for the government to finance the much-needed investments through raising tax and non-tax revenues. According to the 2021 *Final Budget Outcome Report*, NTR collections in 2021 totaled K643.0 million, 44.7% lower than the 2021 Supplementary Budget estimate. Dividend payments in 2021 totaled K530.5 million, 38.3% lower than the estimate.

Recognizing the importance of a viable and overarching regulation to manage NTR, the government tasked the Non-Tax Revenue Division of the Department of Finance to lead a consultative process to draft the Non-Tax Revenue Act (NTRA), which Parliament passed in 2022 and certified in April 2023. This act remedied the unconstitutional sections of the PMMR; stakeholders—such as the Department of Treasury and the Solicitor General's Office—advised the government on how to avoid the legal and fiscal policy concerns that had prompted the Supreme Court to declare the PMMR invalid.

The NTRA permits the regularizing of handling and management of public monies held by public and statutory bodies to raise revenue for the National Budget. It defines all categories of NTR and explains the Non-Tax Revenue Administration Committee's role in overseeing NTR policy for PNG. The NTRA will remit in full all fees and charges collected by statutory bodies and agencies to the Consolidated Revenue Fund before they are appropriated through the government's annual budget. The government's medium-term revenue strategies (MTRSs) that coordinate revenue collection and administration across all tiers of government will support the successful implementation of the NTRA.

The government launched the most recent MTRS (2018–2022) on 28 November 2017. It set a structured and comprehensive reform agenda that supported the government's vision for mobilizing investments and budget resources for services and infrastructure in the health, education, energy, water, communication, and transport sectors. The downturn in business activity during COVID-19 resulted in a decline in government revenues from 16.2% of GDP in 2019 to 14.9% in 2021. Revenues bounced back to 17.2% in 2022 because of higher commodity prices triggered by the Russian invasion of Ukraine and recovery from the COVID-19 pandemic.

Recognizing the development challenges and growing finance needs, the government has committed to bolstering the collection of NTR through the implementation of the NTRA and the planned release of the next MTRS (2023–2027). These two initiatives—combined with enhanced administrative processes and tax collection capacities—will increase land rental and dividend collections, which have been underperforming (Table 3).

NTR fell short by 64.0% when comparing the 2022 supplementary budget to the 2022 budget outcome. This is because both the Bank of Papua New Guinea and Ok Tedi Mining Ltd. remitted no dividend payments in 2022. Kumul Petroleum Holdings paid K300.0 million, which was K400.0 million lower than the supplementary budget estimate. The National Fisheries Authority paid K100.0 million which was 50.0% of the estimate.

The 2023 Budget Strategy Paper includes several revenue policy measures to enhance tax and NTR administration and collection. Digitalization is a key component of the government's revenue-raising strategies as demonstrated by the updating of the Customs Harmonized System. For NTR, improved accountability and reporting arrangements for increasing the collection and remittance of public entity fees, charges, and dividends remain a government priority. An enhanced performance monitoring framework to strengthen NTR collection and build engagement, commitment, and trust among a wide range of stakeholders is a critical policy priority for the government to increase NTR. Moreover, with guidance from the Department of Treasury's Sectoral Policy Division, the government is fine-tuning dividend remittance policies and mitigating the risks that have often delayed the dividend payments remitted by public bodies to the government.

Table 3: Papua New Guinea Other Revenue Collections
(K million)

	2020 Outcome	2021 Supplementary Budget	2021 Outcome	2022 Budget	2022 Supplementary Budget	2022 Outcome	2022 Variation (Supplementary Budget and Outcome)
OTHER REVENUE	**866.1**	**1,163.2**	**643.0**	**1,842.5**	**1,732.7**	**612.5**	**(1,120.2)**
Property Income	**742.1**	**912.7**	**551.8**	**1,305.8**	**1,478.5**	**514.3**	**(964.1)**
Interest	0.0	0.7	0.0	0.7	0.7	0.0	(0.7)
Dividends	718.5	860.0	530.5	1,270.0	1470.0	480.0	(990.0)
Mining Petroleum and Gas Dividends	568.5	600.0	380.5	850.0	1150.0	300.0	(850.0)
Dividends from Statutory Authorities	150.0	260.0	150.0	300.0	300.0	100.0	(200.0)
Dividends from State-Owned Enterprises	0.0	0.0	0.0	120.0	20.0	80.0	60.0
Rent	22.6	52.1	21.3	35.1	7.8	34.3	26.5
Sales of Goods and Services	9.3	35.0	11.4	132.5	14.0	8.4	(5.6)
Admin. fees	4.5	4.6	4.9	99.9	5.8	3.7	(2.1)
Incidental sales by nonmarket establishments	4.8	30.4	6.5	32.6	8.2	4.8	(3.4)
Fines, penalties, and forfeits	2.8	1.8	1.2	1.1	1.1	0.1	(0.9)
Transfers not classified elsewhere	113.0	213.6	78.6	403.2	239.2	89.7	(149.5)
Current transfers	113.0	0.0	78.6	403.2	239.2	89.7	(149.5)

( ) = negative, K = kina.

Source: Government of Papua New Guinea, Department of Treasury. *Final Budget Outcome* (2 years: 2021–2022). Port Moresby.

CONCLUSION

The NTRA provides a legal mechanism to share the remittance of public monies between the government and public and statutory bodies. Its successful implementation will be an important case study of how a country that has been heavily reliant on revenue from its natural resource sector is taking the necessary steps for the government and statutory bodies to transparently and accountably share NTR. The act will ensure that the government and public and statutory bodies share all NTR, estimated by the Department of Finance in May 2023 to potentially amount to as much as K550.0 million annually.

References

Government of Papua New Guinea. 2017. *Medium-Term Revenue Strategy 2018–2022.* Port Moresby.

Government of Papua New Guinea, Department of Treasury. *Final Budget Outcome.* Port Moresby (2 years: 2021–2022).

Government of Papua New Guinea, Department of Treasury. 2022. *2023 Budget Strategy Paper.* Port Moresby.

Tax revenues remained resilient in Samoa despite the pandemic

Lead authors: Yuho Myoda, with contributions from Emmanuel Alano and Maria Melei

Tax revenue in Samoa remained resilient despite the considerable decline in growth during the pandemic. The Samoan economy contracted for three consecutive years since FY2020 (ended 30 June 2020) due to the suspension of international tourism after the country closed its borders in April 2020 (Figure 22). However, domestic demand remained resilient, supported by consecutive fiscal stimulus packages and increased remittances from overseas workers. Tax revenues remained resilient across all three major tax categories. Taxes on goods and services generated the equivalent of 16.2% of nominal GDP in FY2022, buoyed by increased revenue from value-added goods and service tax, partially inflated by higher import prices (Figure 23).

Temporary budget-support grants since FY2020 have boosted government revenue. During FY2012 to FY2019, grant revenue was stable at less than 4.0% of GDP. After the outbreak of the pandemic, this almost doubled to 7.7% of GDP in FY2020, and further to 9.4% of GDP in FY2022, thanks to significant grants from ADB and the World Bank, which became available following the IMF's Poverty Reduction and Growth Trust Fund loans in FY2020.

Figure 22: Demand-Side Contribution to Growth in Samoa

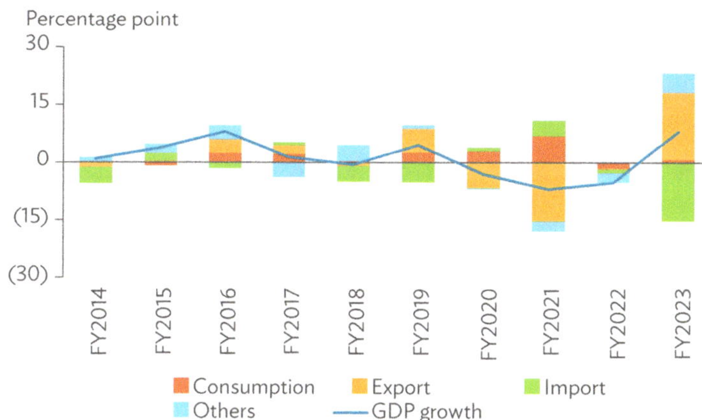

( ) = negative, FY = fiscal year, GDP = gross domestic product.

Note: The fiscal year of the Government of Samoa ends on 30 June.

Source: Government of Samoa, Samoa Bureau of Statistics. Apia.

Figure 23: Samoa Central Government Revenue, by Source

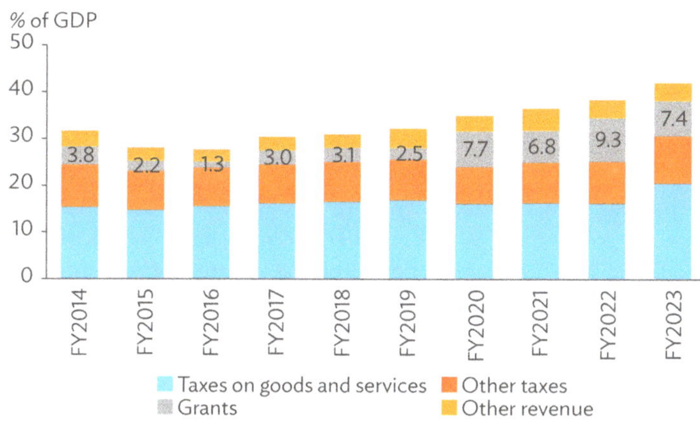

FY = fiscal year, GDP = gross domestic product.

Note: The fiscal year of the Government of Samoa ends on 30 June.

Sources: Government of Samoa, Samoa Bureau of Statistics and Ministry of Finance. Apia.

A raise in excise tax rates was implemented this fiscal year. The increase in taxes on harmful products including tobacco, alcohol, and sugar-sweetened beverages was delayed from FY2021. Given the size of excise tax revenues, the direct revenue gain from the tax hike is relatively limited. Nevertheless, considering the social and health costs caused by the consumption of harmful products in Samoa, strengthening excise taxation will likely have a greater positive fiscal impact by reducing national health expenses in the medium to long term. In addition to the excise tax hike, the Government of Samoa is reviewing non-tax revenues to cover the related costs under elevated prices. Promoting compliance will also remain key to strengthening revenues in the coming years.

Public expenditure continued to increase in line with past trends. Central government spending has constantly increased since FY2018 following spending cuts at a fast pace from FY2015 to FY2017 (Figure 24). Public spending—excluding net acquisition of assets—amounted to 32.2% of GDP in FY2022, up from 21.9% in FY2017. During the pandemic, expenses were driven by grant transfers and subsidies to local governments and state-owned enterprises, such as Samoa Airways, to insulate them from the COVID-19 shock. The general election in FY2021 also added to related expenditure needs during the year. Growth in compensation of employees—which comprises about 40% of total expenses—has picked up due in part to accelerating inflation.

Figure 24: Samoa Central Government Expenditure, by Item

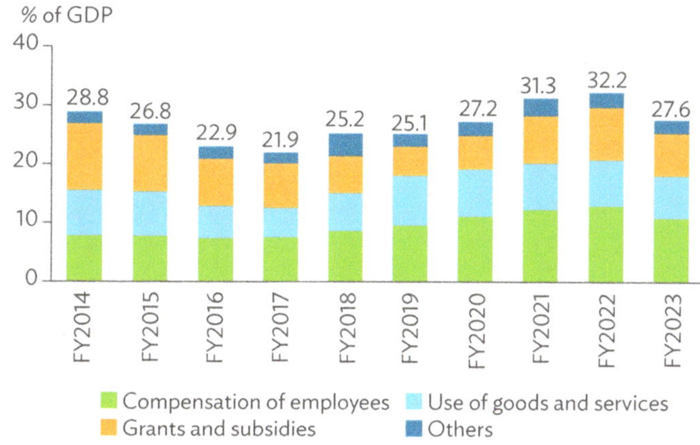

FY = fiscal year, GDP = gross domestic product.

Note: The fiscal year of the Government of Samoa ends on 30 June.

Sources: Government of Samoa, Samoa Bureau of Statistics and Ministry of Finance. Apia.

High prices will likely push up government spending in the coming years. Inflation of 12.0% in FY2023, largely driven by import prices, was the highest in 14 years. The rise in living costs has necessitated an increase in public sector compensation. The government is currently implementing cost-of-living adjustments across all public services, which will be phased in over 3 years through FY2026. This will increase the average compensation of public employees by 5%–10%. Part of the increase in subsidies in FY2023 was accounted for by government support for urgent overseas medical treatment and training for teachers, which is expected to continue. Moreover, Samoa will host the 2024 Commonwealth Heads of Government Meeting in October 2024, which will increase the expenditure requirements in FY2023 and FY2024.

The overall fiscal balance remained in surplus due to grant inflows. The Government of Samoa improved the overall fiscal balance from FY2014 to FY2019 by increasing tax revenues and reducing expenditures (Figure 25). The steady recovery of the economy after the damage from Cyclone Evan in 2012 supported the consolidation. However, a surge in expenditure in response to the global outbreak of COVID-19 led to a fiscal deficit in FY2020 (excluding grants). The fiscal deficit (excluding grants) in percentage to GDP widened to 3.3% in FY2023. Increased foreign grant support allowed the overall government cash flow, including grants, to remain in a surplus of 1.7% of GDP in FY2021, which recovered to 5.4% in FY2022.

Development partner support and buoyant remittances partially offset the widening trade deficits. The abrupt halt in international tourism significantly widened Samoa's goods and services trade deficit from 13.4% of GDP in FY2019 to 40.4% in FY2022. Emergency fiscal grant inflows from external development partners and surging remittances by overseas workers in Australia and New Zealand partially offset the deterioration. Public external debt stood at 33.4% of GDP in FY2023, down from its pre-pandemic figure of 43.7% in FY2019.

Figure 25: Samoa Fiscal Balance

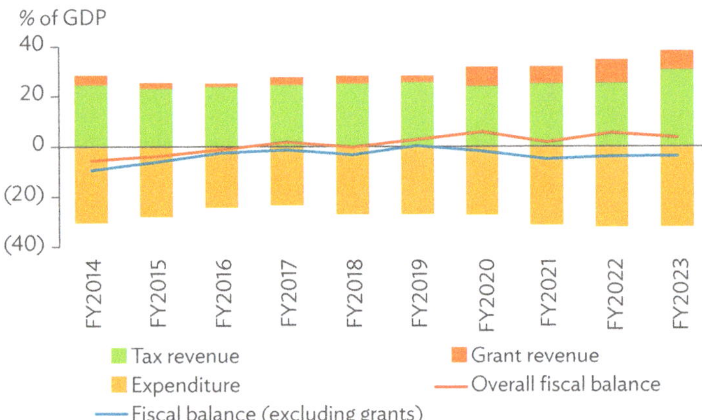

( ) = negative, FY = fiscal year, GDP = gross domestic product.

Note: The fiscal year of the Government of Samoa ends on 30 June.

Sources: Government of Samoa, Samoa Bureau of Statistics and Ministry of Finance. Apia.

Further mobilizing tax revenue is warranted in the medium term. To secure sufficient fiscal space to meet the increasing spending demands for sustainable growth, the government needs to shore up tax revenues. As the general sales tax rate is already relatively high at 15% compared to peer economies, reviewing the scope of zero-rating and exemptions may be an important component of expanding revenue. Reviewing exemptions and deductions and efforts to improve compliance will also be relevant for other tax categories including corporate income tax and customs duties.

Reforming retail energy pricing can promote efficient consumption and strengthen financial resources. Price subsidies, including VAT exemption, are generally less efficiently targeted to mitigate the regressivity of VAT and support less-wealthy households who are more vulnerable to price increases. The government can review its price subsidy and partially replace this with transfers to the vulnerable households. Samoa's current excise tax rates on fossil fuels are low, leaving retail prices for vehicle gas and kerosene lower than its Pacific peers (Pacific Regional Data Repository 2019). Raising fuel excise tax rates—with proper cushions for consumers from vulnerable groups— would save fossil fuel consumption and strengthen revenues. Since Samoa relies almost exclusively on crude oil imports for its primary

energy sources, optimizing the consumption of fossil fuels will likely reduce pressure on the balance of payments. For the same reason, utility tariffs, especially for electricity, should have a flexible mechanism to reflect input costs and secure the state-owned power corporation to cover the costs of maintenance and investment.

The government needs to review emergency expenses and keep pursuing grant funding for capital investment. The fiscal surplus during the pandemic period was due to a temporary increase in inflows of general assistance grant funds, which are expected to decline to previous levels in the coming years. In addition, the country's vulnerability to climate change will likely increase the fiscal demand for mitigation and adaptation. The government needs to review and phase out emergency expenses such as financial support to state-owned enterprises and pursue grant funding where possible.

Skilled labor shortages and increasing noncommunicable disease cases pose a risk to long-term growth. Apart from the adverse impacts of climate change, the issue of labor emigration—particularly to Australia and New Zealand—has long-term implications for the availability of domestic semi-skilled workers. The extension of seasonal labor mobility programs to various service sectors from originally seasonal agricultural work has significantly increased Samoan overseas workers in Australia and New Zealand. Although their increased remittances to Samoa supported the economy during the pandemic period, the prospect of these workers settling down in these countries could reduce the future workforce of Samoa. In parallel with efforts to improve the quality of education, the Samoan government will need to create job opportunities through economic diversification. The increasing number of patients with noncommunicable diseases such as cardiovascular disease, may have adverse impacts on growth by hurting the future labor force and reducing fiscal space through increased subsidies for medical care.

References

ADB. Asian Development Outlook Database (accessed October 2023).

S. Boila. 2023. Budget 2023-2024: 5% Increase on Alcohol and Tobacco Excise Duty. FBC News. 30 June.

Ch-aviation. 2023. Samoa Airways wants more funding as gov't takes over loan. 8 August.

Development Policy Centre, Australian National University. 2023. We Want the Forest but Fear the Spirits: Labour Mobility Predicaments in Samoa. *DevPolicyBlog*. 10 July.

Government of Samoa, Central Bank of Samoa. 2023. Quarterly Bulletin: Government Finance (accessed November 2023).

Government of Samoa, Samoa Bureau of Statistics. 2023. *Government Finance Statistics Report (March Quarter 2023)*.

Government of Samoa. Ministry of Finance. 2023. Quarterly Economic Review 100 (Third Quarter FY 2022/23).

Pacific Regional Data Repository. 2019. *Pacific Fuel Price Monitor (January–March 2019)*.

Natural hazards increased Tonga's dependence on development assistance

Lead authors: Yuho Myoda and Emmanuel Alano

Increased external grants, with resilient tax revenue, maintained Tonga's overall revenue. The Tongan economy contracted for 2 consecutive years in FY2021 (ended on 30 June) and FY2022 after the global outbreak of COVID-19. However, domestic demand, supported by strong remittances, remained resilient, resulting in an increase in tax revenue to GDP ratio during this period (Figure 26). At the same time, the government has been improving tax collection efficiency by adopting various ICT-based tools. For instance, retail stores will soon be required to install an electronic sales register system to record and transmit real-time sales information to the Ministry of Revenue and Customs. Efforts are also underway at the border, where a single-window electronic system for customs clearance and X-ray machines have been installed. These are expected to reduce errors related to tax reporting and improve taxpayer compliance by reducing costs and providing partial automation of data collection (ADB 2022). With resilient tax revenue and increased development assistance, total revenue (including grants) as a percentage of GDP remained higher than pre-pandemic levels (Figure 27). Grants comprised 43.9% of total revenue in FY2019, rising to 51.1% in FY2023.

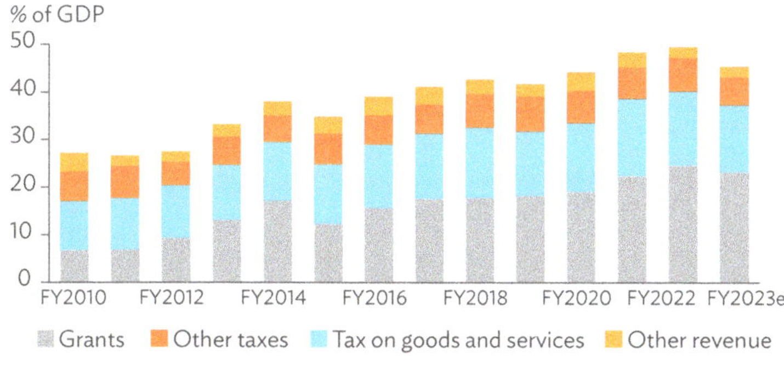

Figure 26: Tonga Central Government Revenue, by Source

e = estimate, FY = fiscal year, GDP = gross domestic product.

Note: The fiscal year of the Government of Tonga ends on 30 June.

Sources: ADB estimates; United Nations University World Institute for Development Economics Research. 2023. Government Revenue Dataset (accessed October 2023); Government of Tonga, Ministry of Finance. 2023. *Budget Statement.* Nuku'alofa; Government of Tonga, Statistics Department. 2023. *Government Finance Statistics.* Nuku'alofa; and International Monetary Fund. 2023. *World Economic Outlook.* Washington, DC (October).

The pandemic response increased government current expenditures in FY2021. Prior to the pandemic, Tonga had been controlling the growth of government spending below its economic growth. As a result, total central government expenditure held steady at 25.9% of GDP in FY2019 compared to 26.9% in FY2015 (Figure 27). In FY2020, the COVID-19 pandemic flipped the trend, causing large increases in government employee compensation and other intermediate input costs. Total spending increased to 29.6% of GDP in FY2020 and to 36.9% in FY2021.

In FY2022, the tsunami following the eruption of the Hunga Tonga-Hunga Ha'apai volcanic eruption, and the first community spread of COVID-19 caused delays in many infrastructure projects resulting in a slight decline in the expenditure-to-GDP ratio to 36.4%.

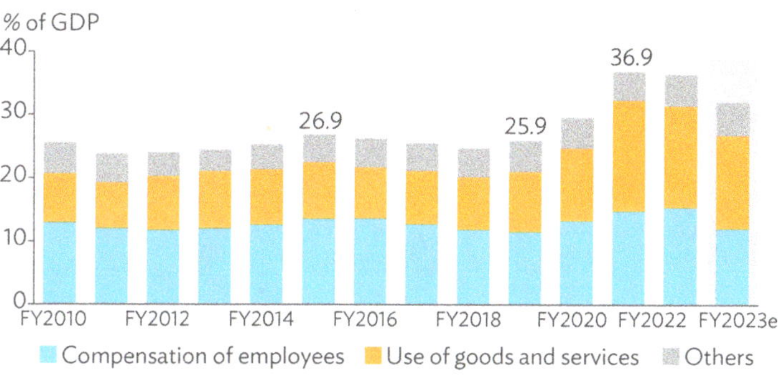

Figure 27: Tonga Central Government Expenditure, by Item

e = estimate, FY = fiscal year, GDP = gross domestic product.

Note: The fiscal year of the Government of Tonga ends on 30 June.

Sources: ADB estimates; Government of Tonga, Ministry of Finance. 2023. *Budget Statement.* Nuku'alofa; Government of Tonga, Statistics Department. 2023. *Government Finance Statistics.* Nuku'alofa; and International Monetary Fund. 2023. *World Economic Outlook.* Washington, DC (October).

The budget balance fell into deficit in FY2021 and FY2022 due to pandemic-related expenditures. Through tax revenue stabilization measures and expenditure control efforts, the Government of Tonga maintained a budget surplus during FY2017–FY2020 but a significant increase in pandemic-related spending pushed it into the red in FY2021 (Figure 28). The public-debt-to-GDP ratio started rising again in FY2020. When the government started its fiscal consolidation efforts in FY2016, the ratio was almost 50.0% and stabilized at 41.3% in FY2019. Despite the deferment of debt repayments under the G20 Debt Service Suspension Initiative, total government debt outstanding stood at 44.4% in FY2022.

Remittances from residents working abroad increased during the pandemic. The services trade deficit expanded in FY2021 due to the shutdown of the tourism industry in the wake of the COVID-19 pandemic. However, remittances from emigrant workers increased significantly to 39.2% of GDP in FY2023 from 29.9% in FY2019. Higher remittances, together with the increased support from development partners, prevented the current account deficit from widening amid downward pressures on the trade balance (Figure 29).

Tax administration improvements will likely remain the focus of domestic resource mobilization. Tonga's consumption tax rate has been at 15% since FY2005, among the highest in the subregion. Given the current focus on reconstruction from the damage by the volcanic eruption, a further increase in the tax rate is not feasible. The ratio of total goods and services sales tax revenues, including consumption tax revenues, to GDP has also stabilized at an average of 14.7% from FY2017 to FY2022. Domestic resource mobilization efforts will continue to focus on improving tax administration, which would boost compliance by reducing tax payment and collection costs.

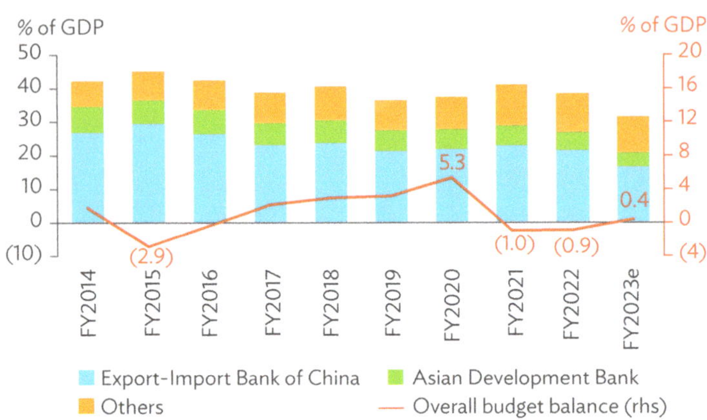

Figure 28: Tonga Budget Balance and Debt

( ) = negative, e = estimate, FY = fiscal year, GDP = gross domestic product, rhs = right-hand scale.

Note: The fiscal year of the Government of Tonga ends on 30 June.

Sources: ADB estimates; Government of Tonga, Ministry of Finance. 2023. *Budget Statement.* Nuku'alofa; National Reserve Bank of Tonga. 2023. *Quarterly Bulletin.* Nuku'alofa; and International Monetary Fund. 2023. *World Economic Outlook.* Washington, DC (October).

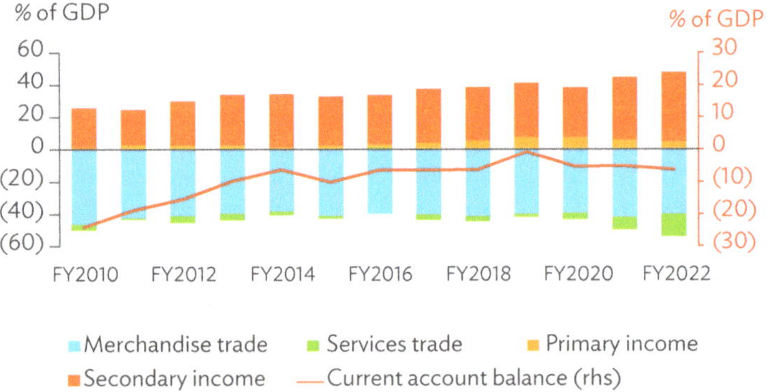

Figure 29: Tonga Current Account Balance, by Components

( ) = negative, FY = fiscal year, GDP = gross domestic product, rhs = right hand scale.

Note: The fiscal year of the Government of Tonga ends on 30 June.

Source: International Monetary Fund and CEIC Data Company (accessed November 2023).

Value-added tax exemptions need to be reviewed to narrow the tax gap. Despite the high consumption tax rate in Tonga relative to the rest of the subregion, significant exemptions have hindered Tonga from achieving its tax capacity. The exemptions are intended to mitigate the regressivity of the VAT. However, reducing prices via price subsidies or tax exemptions is less efficient than targeted cash transfers to vulnerable households. The most significant VAT exemption applies to the state-owned electricity firm's consumption of diesel fuel, which will likely generate additional revenue of more than 1% of GDP if abandoned. Reducing tax exemptions will likely decrease administrative costs by simplifying the tax code and collection process.

Tonga will continue to rely heavily on grants in the coming years. Damage caused by previous disasters necessitates considerable expenditure on reconstruction in the next few years. As the untapped short-term tax potential is limited, this large fiscal demand will only likely be satisfied by grants. However, grant support from development partners is expected to revert to historical trend levels as assistance programs normalize post-COVID-19. Grants currently far exceed tax revenues, accounting for as much as 23.2% of GDP in FY2023, compared to 18.3% in FY2019. In parallel with mobilizing domestic tax revenues and streamlining the existing expenditures, the Government of Tonga will likely need to secure new grants beyond the end of already committed support to continue to make necessary fixed investments.

In the medium term, a further levy on energy consumption can raise additional funds. The removal of the VAT levy exemption for the state electricity company will provide immediate benefits to revenue collection while the government could also consider other adjustments. The current flat electricity tariff could be reformed to become more progressive so that the electricity firm and the government can increase revenue to cover the costs of necessary investments for the transition to cleaner energy sources. In the medium term, taxing fossil fuels—especially gas and kerosene—can generate additional resources for climate finance even under the constraint of limited administrative capacity as it only requires taxing a small number of importers (ADB 2022). However, as the retail prices of gasoline and kerosene in Tonga are not particularly low compared to peer economies in the Pacific, sufficient mitigation measures—including financial support for vulnerable households—should be considered in conjunction with the introduction of fuel taxes.

References

Asian Development Bank (ADB). 2022. *Asian Development Outlook: Mobilizing Taxes for Development.* March.

ADB. 2023. Asian Development Outlook Database (accessed October 2023).

Government of Tonga, Ministry of Finance. *Budget Statement.* Nuku'alofa (9 years: 2015–2023).

Government of Tonga, Ministry of Revenue and Customs. 2023. Consumption Tax Overview. Nuku'alofa.

Government of Tonga, Statistics Department. 2023. Government Finance Statistics (accessed October 2023).

International Monetary Fund (IMF). 2022. Tonga 2022 Article IV Consultation. *IMF Country Report.* No. 22/282. Washington, DC.

IMF. 2023. World Economic Outlook Database (accessed October 2023).

National Reserve Bank of Tonga. 2023. Quarterly Bulletin (accessed November 2023).

United Nations University World Institute for Development Economics Research (UNU-WIDER). 2023. *Government Revenue Dataset* (accessed October 2023).

T. Wainibalagi. 2019. *Pacific Energy News Updates.* The Pacific Community. 20 June.

The Role of Domestic Resource Mobilization and Financing Needs in the Pacific

Domestic resource mobilization (DRM) has been a long-standing challenge for Pacific developing member countries (DMCs) that have historically relied on grants from development partners and revenues from a few activities such as fisheries and tourism.

The external shock from the coronavirus disease (COVID-19) pandemic, international border closures, declining commodity exports, and limited financing options have compounded the difficulty of supporting inclusive and resilient growth in the subregion. Rising fiscal deficits during the pandemic have led to a surge in public debt, further squeezing limited fiscal space.[1] Post-COVID-19, governments are focusing on creating extra fiscal space by raising taxes, securing grants, and cutting lower-priority expenditures.

The Pacific DMCs' economic challenges are further complicated by the development-climate nexus, reflecting their vulnerability to external shocks from climate change and disasters triggered by natural hazards. Many of the Pacific DMCs face substantial constraints in enhancing the resilience of infrastructure to disasters and achieving the United Nations' Sustainable Development Goals (SDGs). Additionally, their economies' small size and remoteness limit government capacity to mitigate the impact of external shocks emanating from climate change and natural disasters.

To achieve the SDGs and support more inclusive and sustainable growth, the Pacific DMCs need to create additional fiscal space through DRM and improving expenditure efficiency. The financing needs to upgrade and adapt the necessary climate-resilient infrastructure are massive, and the Pacific DMCs will have to explore a variety of financing options to bankroll the desired investments. The financing gap has even increased because of the COVID-19 pandemic. In the post-COVID-19 environment, the Pacific DMCs will have to exert extra effort in mobilizing additional resources to support investments and improve the quality of public services.

The Pacific DMCs have performed relatively well compared to other emerging market economies on indicators such as education, electricity, water, and sanitation services. Nevertheless, the level of additional spending needed to meet selected SDG targets from 2019 to 2030 is estimated to be 6.7% of 2030 gross domestic product (GDP) per annum (Tiedemann et al. 2021). Moreover, investments required to upgrade and build physical infrastructure are estimated at an additional 3.7% of 2030 GDP per year. The average spending needs for existing and planned infrastructure related to climate change are estimated at 3.1% of 2030 GDP per year and spending needs for investment and maintenance costs for coastal protection are estimated at 3.1%–4.3% of 2030 GDP (Sy et al. 2022).

These spending needs are enormous and underscore the importance of maintaining adequate fiscal buffers. However, limited fiscal space and few funding options make it challenging for the Pacific DMCs to support SDG-related investments. Although some of the required investments can be financed domestically, DRM alone will be insufficient to meet these financing needs. The Pacific DMCs also need external technical and financial support to provide ample fiscal space to ensure progress.

Given the high risk of debt distress in many Pacific DMCs, the scope for additional borrowing is further curtailed (Sy et al. 2022). For example, in 2019, 6 out of 14 Pacific DMCs were at high risk of debt distress, while another 3 were classified medium-risk. With the COVID-19 external shock, the number of countries at high risk of debt distress increased further to 7 in 2020 and 8 in 2021, while 3 economies remained at medium-risk. The latest information reveals that during 2022 and 2023, 7 countries are still at high risk of debt distress and 3 countries are classified medium-risk (Figure 1).

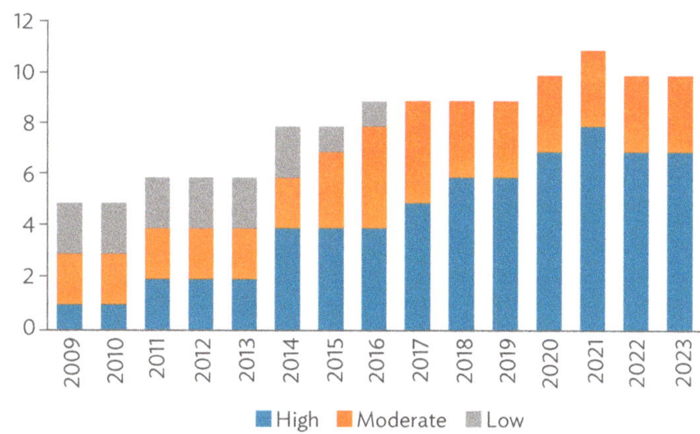

Figure 1: Number of Pacific Developing Member Countries at Risk of Debt Distress

Notes:
1. Countries included are the Federated States of Micronesia (FSM), Fiji, Kiribati, the Marshall Islands, Nauru, Palau, Papua New Guinea, Samoa, Solomon Islands, Tonga, Tuvalu, and Vanuatu.
2. Rating for the FSM is based on 2021 assessment.
3. No IMF debt sustainability analysis rating available for the Cook Islands and Niue.

Sources: International Monetary Fund (IMF) Article IV (various issues); and M. Sy et al. 2022. Funding the Future: Tax Revenue Mobilization in the Pacific Island Countries. *Departmental Paper No. 2022/015*. Washington, DC: IMF.

Table 1: Fiscal Space Indicators for Pacific Developing Member Countries

Indicators	Unit	2015	2016	2017	2018	2019	2020	2021	2022
General government gross debt	% of GDP	52.3	54.8	55.0	54.9	55.7	66.7	65.6	62.8
Primary balance	% of GDP	(1.3)	(1.6)	(0.3)	0.5	(0.3)	(5.2)	(2.7)	(1.2)
Fiscal balance	% of GDP	(2.4)	(2.7)	(1.5)	(0.6)	(1.4)	(6.3)	(3.9)	(2.6)
General government gross debt	% of average tax revenues	397.0	454.1	463.7	448.1	452.0	555.5	533.0	494.2
Fiscal balance	% of average tax revenues	(29.7)	(44.6)	(18.2)	(4.8)	(16.2)	(66.7)	(35.6)	(1.2)
General government gross debt	% of 10-year moving average GDP	69.4	72.1	75.4	76.3	76.4	88.6	94.4	97.5
Fiscal balance	% of 10-year moving average GDP	(3.2)	(3.5)	(2.1)	(1.1)	(2.2)	(7.6)	(5.2)	(3.4)
Concessional external debt stocks	% of external public debt	33.8	33.2	32.3	31.8	31.9	32.4	32.6	...
Total external debt stocks	% of GDP	152.5	153.0	155.8	144.1	146.4	160.2	139.5	169.6
Short-term external debt stocks	% of total	19.0	18.2	18.5	18.5	18.1	17.8	17.8	24.7

( ) = negative, ... = data not available, GDP = gross domestic product.

Source: Computations based on M. Kose et al. 2022. A Cross-Country Database of Fiscal Space. *Journal of International Money and Finance.* 128 (November): Article 102682.

Given the limited room for additional borrowing, the onus shifts toward mobilizing more domestic resources. The COVID-19 shock has squeezed the already limited fiscal space and highlighted the importance of DRM. An evaluation of multiple macro-fiscal indicators in the Pacific DMCs indicates a significant deterioration in fiscal space during the pre- and post-COVID-19 environment (Table 1).

The fiscal deficit, which averaged around 1.7% of GDP in 2015–2019, surged sharply to 4.3% of GDP during 2020–2022. Meanwhile, the primary deficit increased from 0.6% of GDP to 3.0% of GDP, pushing the debt-to-GDP ratio from 54.5% in 2015–2019 to 65.0% in 2020–2022. Likewise, total external debt stocks in the Pacific DMCs have increased from 150.4% of GDP during 2015–2019 to 156.4% of GDP by 2020–2022. Even adjusting for volatility in GDP growth, the ratios of debt and fiscal deficit to the 10-year moving average of GDP also corroborate these findings.

This analysis validates reduction in fiscal space of the Pacific DMCs between 2015 and 2022, and the importance of mobilizing more domestic resources. With non-tax revenues and grants accounting for about 56% of Pacific DMCs' total revenue, DRM should focus on enhancing tax revenue collections. Although tax-to-GDP ratio in the Pacific DMCs improved from 19.2% in 2015 to 20.1% in 2022, it remains dominated by indirect taxes, which account for about 68% of total revenues. Additionally, value-added tax (VAT) is not fully exploited in the Pacific subregion. Five out of 12 Pacific DMCs do not have a VAT system in place, resulting in tax collection which is about 50% of its potential VAT (Kose et al. 2022).

DRM is crucial for governments to create the fiscal space to fund public investments and deliver public services. The rapid rise in fiscal deficits and elevated levels of public debt in the aftermath of the COVID-19 shock have constrained the policymakers' ability to respond to the economic crisis. The pandemic has become a painful reminder for governments and policymakers across the globe of the need to maintain sufficient fiscal buffers to support macroeconomic stability. Empirical evidence shows that the effectiveness of fiscal stimulus reduces when debt is elevated, underscoring the need to improve fiscal positions to mitigate the impacts of macroeconomic shocks (Brinca et al. 2016).

Ensuring a sustainable fiscal stance requires maintaining ample fiscal space to implement growth-enhancing spending while implementing tax reforms to better mobilize domestic resources. To achieve inclusive and sustainable growth, it is equally important to have a consistent policy framework anchoring long-term expectations while allowing decisive short- to-medium-term accommodation whenever necessary. Credible policy commitment and enduring prudent management practices would give fiscal policy the flexibility to support economic activities and help mobilize DRM to scale up productive investments (Gaspar et al. 2016). In Pacific DMCs, whose economies remain vulnerable to shocks and face reduced fiscal space, policy credibility is the key to the success of fiscal stimulus. A continuously rising public debt-to-GDP ratio may pose a threat to fiscal sustainability, while a clearly defined fiscal framework can help improve the public sector balance sheet in the event of macro-fiscal shocks.

By systematically relating policy objectives and instruments over time, a consistent and coordinated policy framework can provide governments with more policy space to fund public investments as well as deliver public services. The quality of these public investments and services is crucial to providing an enabling business environment for the private sector and increasing potential output. Evidence suggests that, for countries facing sizable infrastructure gaps, a permanent increase in government investment of 1% relative to baseline GDP could enhance private investment from 0.3% to 0.6% and support productivity-led growth. The resulting higher economic growth can create future policy space by raising more government revenues and reducing debt distress (IMF 2015).

The results of an IMF (Akitoby et al. 2018) study that analyzed 55 episodes of large tax revenue increases in low-income countries (LICs) and emerging markets (EMs) suggest that the success of DRM crucially depends upon indirect tax collections, policy measures, and multi-pronged tax administration reforms. Improving compliance and reducing exemptions, including eliminating tax holidays, were also found to be instrumental in broadening the tax base for both direct and indirect taxes, thereby enhancing government revenues. Further, introducing and simplifying VAT and increasing its efficiency can also lead to significant revenue gains. LICs and EMs improved their average C-efficiency[2] from 0.25 and 0.47, respectively, in 2000 to 0.36 and 0.57 in 2015, contributing to increased VAT revenues during the period. The analysis also suggests that successful DRM is frequently supported by a combination of parallel revenue administration and tax policy reforms.

As the Pacific DMCs' economies develop, there is plenty of room for enhancing direct tax revenues. Their small and dispersed populations, limited economic diversification, and weak absorptive capacities constrain their collective ability to raise tax collections. Addressing these constraints through capacity-building and expanding the tax base can be instrumental in enhancing the tax potential in these countries. For example, an IMF study utilizing tax frontier analysis suggests that the additional tax revenues that the Pacific DMCs can collect by addressing their administrative, monitoring, and enforcement capabilities are as high as 3% of GDP (Sy et al. 2022). These are quite significant gains and—if utilized properly—can help finance investments needed to achieve SDGs. The study further reveals that the magnitude of the untapped taxes varies across Pacific DMCs. Tourism-dependent countries such as Fiji and Samoa, which are performing relatively well in terms of DRM, have the least potential to further increase total revenues through direct taxes. Countries with Compacts of Free Association with the United States—the Federated States of Micronesia, the Marshall Islands, and Palau—still have huge potential to further enhance government revenue through direct taxes. Commodity exports also have a large unexploited tax potential.

Although the Pacific DMCs have significant potential to further enhance tax revenues, it is contingent upon addressing the key constraints inhibiting DRM. For example, improving government effectiveness, enhancing the quality of public services, improving the quality of policy formulation and implementation, and enhancing the administrative capacity of tax collectors are crucial in minimizing the tax gap and mobilizing additional domestic resources. Optimizing revenue by modernizing and reforming the tax administration could enhance the capacity of governments to collect more taxes. Since most Pacific DMCs are facing staff shortages and capacity issues resulting in tax avoidance and evasion, enhancing the absorptive capacity of the tax administration could bridge the gap and contribute to additional revenue collections. Because the current VAT systems are not adequate, reforms to improve these systems could also help reduce informality and enhance DRM.

Lead author: Kaukab Naqvi

Endnotes

[1]   Fiscal space is defined as room in a government's budget that allows it to provide resources for a desired purpose without jeopardizing the sustainability of its financial position or the stability of the economy.

[2]   C-efficiency is the ratio of actual VAT to potential VAT if all final consumption were taxed at the standard rate.

References

B. Akitoby et al. 2018. Tax Revenue Mobilization Episodes in Emerging Markets and Low-Income Countries: Lessons from a New Dataset Making Public Investment More Efficient. *Working Paper No. 2018/234.* Washington, DC: IMF.

P. Brinca et al. 2016. Fiscal multipliers in the 21st century. *Journal of Monetary Economics.* 77 (February). pp 53–69.

V. Gaspar et al. 2016. Macroeconomic Management When Policy Space Is Constrained: A Comprehensive, Consistent, and Coordinated Approach to Economic Policy. *Discussion Note.* No 2016/009. Washington, DC: IMF.

International Monetary Fund. 2015. Making Public Investment More Efficient. Washington, DC: IMF.

M. Kose et al. 2022. A Cross-Country Database of Fiscal Space. *Journal of International Money and Finance.* 128 (November). Article 102682.

W. Leal Filho et al. 2022. An assessment of requirements in investments, new technologies, and infrastructures to achieve the SDGs. *Environmental Sciences Europe.* 34:58.

M. Sy et al. 2022. Funding the Future: Tax Revenue Mobilization in the Pacific Island Countries. *Departmental Paper No. 2022/015.* Washington, DC: IMF.

J. Tiedemann et al. 2021. Meeting the Sustainable Development Goals in Small Developing States with Climate Vulnerabilities: Cost and Financing. *Working Paper No. 2021/062.* Washington, DC: IMF.

Tax Administration Reform through Digital Transformation

CHALLENGES FACING TAX REGIMES IN THE PACIFIC

Recent global economic shocks have required Pacific governments to implement fiscal policies to support their people and economies. The resulting deterioration in their fiscal positions has been accompanied by the loss of revenues, higher debt, and increased vulnerability to future economic shocks. The coronavirus disease (COVID-19) pandemic also exposed the need for substantial new investments in health systems, education, and social protection.

Pacific developing member countries (DMCs) continue to steadily recover from recent shocks and grow. The subregion is forecast to grow by 3.5% in 2023—faster than 3.3% projected earlier—and 2.9% in 2024 (ADB 2023). However, recovery remains fragile. DMCs are also facing significant additional spending needs related to achieving the UN Sustainable Development Goals and the rising costs of climate change adaptation. According to the International Monetary Fund (IMF), the additional cost for Pacific economies to meet selected Sustainable Development Goal targets in 2030 averages approximately 6.3% of 2030 gross domestic product (GDP). Among small developing states in general, annual additional spending for physical infrastructure would need to increase by 3.1% of GDP per year to make existing and planned infrastructure climate resilient (Sy et al. 2022).

In addition to external concessional financing, supporting economic development in the Pacific requires these economies to mobilize domestic resources. This is important to maintain ample fiscal space and to reduce economic vulnerabilities in times of crisis. Revenue also needs to come from more predictable sources. Several Pacific governments receive a substantial portion of their revenue from non-tax sources—such as fishing license fees, trust fund investments, and official development assistance—which tend to be unpredictable or beyond government control compared to revenue from tax sources (Sy et al. 2022).

Securing adequate and sustainable tax revenues has been challenging for these governments. The average tax-to-GDP ratio for Pacific countries in 2021 was 18.5%, which is comparable to those of other small states and Caribbean countries,[1] above the threshold of 15.0%, but well below the Organisation for Economic Co-operation and Development average of 34.1% (OECD 2023).[2] The average tax gap—the difference between the total taxes owed and the total tax revenue collected—in the Pacific subregion is about 3.0% of GDP (Sy et al. 2022). These statistics suggest that domestic resource mobilization (DRM) should be a major strategic priority for Pacific governments.

There are various ways that Pacific economies can secure additional resources through enhanced DRM. Many DMCs over the last few years have undertaken reforms on broad tax policy and administration matters—with support from development partners—to strengthen DRM (Pacific Financial Technical Assistance Centre 2023).

One promising reform is modernizing the tax administration through digitalization, which can improve tax administration efficiency, transparency, and productivity. Digitalization is also a key component of a medium-term revenue strategy and DRM, in general.

DIGITALIZATION OF TAX ADMINISTRATION

Research suggests that digitalization of tax administration has a range of benefits for both tax administrations and taxpayers, including lower administrative and compliance costs, reduced corruption, and enhanced tax compliance, all of which lead to an increase in tax revenue collection (Asian Development Bank Institute 2022).

It is also widely acknowledged that information and communication technology (ICT) systems are required for core tax administration functions, which include taxpayer registration, filing and payment of taxes, taxpayer services, and processing (ADB 2020a).

While most of the world's tax administrations have implemented some form of ICT system, the rate of adoption in many developing economies lags (Economic and Social Commission for Asia and the Pacific 2022). Most tax administrations in the Pacific have embarked on some level of digitalization—in most cases, e-registration, and e-filing. However, there do remain a couple of manual and paper-based processes. Table 2 sets out the data reported by Pacific DMC tax administrations for fiscal year 2021 regarding the use of technologies in their day-to-day operations or in the course of being implemented.

Implementing digital reforms can be a significant challenge for any tax administration, particularly for those in developing economies. Challenges include a lack of political support, ineffective coordination with relevant stakeholders, limited capacity in human and technology resources, and a lack of an overall digital strategy. For economies in the Pacific, these challenges are compounded by internet connectivity and infrastructure limitations, weak ICT systems in other government departments and institutions, and limited taxpayer access to internet services. Additionally, funding and investment in tax administration by Pacific governments are limited (ADB, forthcoming).

A forthcoming ADB report finds that most tax administrations in the Pacific subregion could make greater use of technology to support their delivery of tax administration operations. During fiscal years 2018 to 2021, four DMCs reported spending less than 5% per annum of total operating expenditure on information ICT expenditures, three DMCs reported average expenditure of more than 10%, and Nauru and Samoa did not report any data (ADB,

Table 2: Use of Technology in Pacific Tax Administration

Economy	Operational ICT Solutions of the Tax Administration are...			Status with Use of Innovative Technologies			
	Custom built	On premises commercial off the shelf	Software-as-a-Service (i.e., cloud-based)	Data Science/ Analytics Tools	Robotics Process Automation	Cloud computing	Whole of Government ID System
Cook Islands	No	Yes	No	Implementing	Not Applicable	Not Applicable	Not Applicable
Federated States of Micronesia	No	No	No	Not Applicable	Not Applicable	Not Applicable	Not Applicable
Fiji	Yes	No	No	In Place	Not Applicable	In Place	Not Applicable
Kiribati	No	No	No	Not Applicable	Not Applicable	Not Applicable	Not Applicable
Marshall Islands, Republic of the	No	No	No	Not Applicable	Not Applicable	Not Applicable	Not Applicable
Nauru	No	No	No	Not Applicable	Not Applicable	Not Applicable	Not Applicable
Niue	No	No	No	Not Applicable	Not Applicable	Not Applicable	Not Applicable
Palau	Yes	No	No	Not Applicable	Not Applicable	Not Applicable	Not Applicable
Papua New Guinea	Yes	Yes	No	Implementing	Implementing	Implementing	Not Applicable
Samoa	Yes	Yes	Yes	Not Applicable	Not Applicable	Not Applicable	Not Applicable
Solomon Islands	No	Yes	No	Not Applicable	Not Applicable	Not Applicable	Not Applicable
Tonga	No	Yes	No	Not Applicable	Not Applicable	Not Applicable	Not Applicable
Tuvalu	No	Yes	No	Not Applicable	Not Applicable	Not Applicable	Not Applicable
Vanuatu	No	No	No	Not Applicable	Not Applicable	Not Applicable	In Place

ICT = information and communication technology.

Sources: Revenue Administrations Fiscal Information Tool. International Survey on Revenue Administration (accessed 19 October 2023); and Survey Results from the Pacific Financial Technical Assistance Centre, Pacific Islands Tax Administrators Association.

forthcoming) (Figure 2).[3] As a comparison, Australia and New Zealand both reported expenditures averaging more than 14% per annum of total operating expenditures.

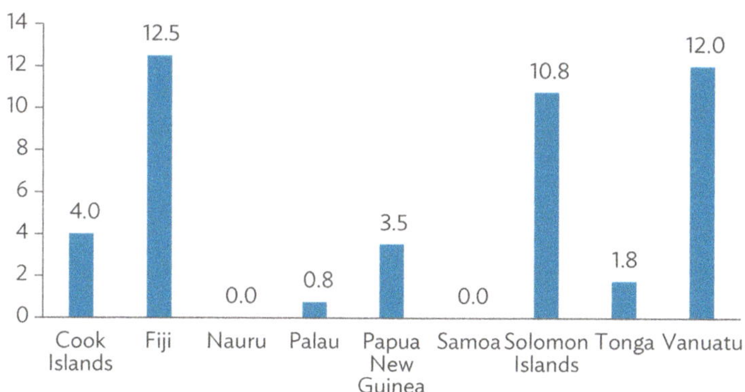

Figure 2: Pacific Average Information and Communication Technology Operating Expenditure, FY2018–FY2021

FY = fiscal year.

Note: The fiscal year ends on 30 June for the Cook Islands, Nauru, Samoa, and Tonga; 31 July for Fiji; 30 September for Palau; and 31 December elsewhere.

Sources: Revenue Administrations Fiscal Information Tool. International Survey on Revenue Administration (accessed 19 October 2023); and Survey Results from the Pacific Financial Technical Assistance Centre, Pacific Islands Tax Administrators Association.

Despite the many challenges, improving the functions of tax administration through digital tools should be part of a government's DRM plan as it can play a key role in improving revenue collection.

Recognizing the importance of digitally transforming tax administration, ADB and the Asia Pacific Tax Hub (APTH) have taken several steps to support ADB's DMCs on their transformational journey.

ADB AND THE ASIA PACIFIC TAX HUB

ADB is committed to achieving a prosperous, inclusive, resilient, and sustainable Asia and the Pacific while sustaining efforts to eradicate extreme poverty. Operational priority 6 set out in ADB's Strategy 2030 covers strengthening governance capacity matters including DRM and international tax cooperation (ITC).

To address this operational priority, ADB officially launched the APTH in May 2021. The APTH provides an open and inclusive platform for strategic policy dialogue, knowledge sharing and dissemination, and development coordination among ADB, its DMCs, and development partners.

Through the APTH, DMCs are assisted in developing tailored DRM and ITC goals and strategies using three building blocks: (i) formulating a medium-term revenue strategy; (ii) developing a roadmap for the digitalization of tax administration; and

(iii) effective participation in ITC initiatives. The work of the ATPH also allows ADB to mainstream DRM and ITC in its technical assistance and policy-based lending (ADB 2020b).

Given the importance of digitally transforming a tax administration and the many challenges DMCs may face, ADB published a digital tax administration transformation manual in 2022.

In addition—to respond to the strong demand for capacity and knowledge development in the digitalization of tax administration—ADB and the APTH—in collaboration with development partners—organized several regional events on this topic.

ADB and the APTH are also ready to provide country-specific support to DMCs. Such support is already underway for Bhutan's Department of Revenue and Customs and Maldives Inland Revenue Administration.

DIGITAL TAX ADMINISTRATION TRANSFORMATION MANUAL

The digital tax administration transformation manual is designed to support DMCs on a digital transformation of tax administration. It sets out the key areas that should be considered and analyzed when deciding whether and how far to go in the transformation. These include:

(i)   the possible reasons for undergoing a transformational reform,
(ii)   the elements needed to build a digital transformation roadmap,
(iii)   an outline of the potential endpoints or targets,
(iv)   the potential risks and challenges in undertaking reform, and
(v)   the measures to assess the impact of a digital transformation reform (ADB 2022).

A successful digital transformation reform requires a clear vision and target, thorough organization, and effective implementation. For this reason, DMCs are recommended to develop a digital transformation roadmap. The roadmap will ensure that the various workstreams involved in a transformational reform are coordinated, as well as set out an implementation plan with a timeline.

To build this roadmap, a DMC will need to complete several steps (Figure 3).

As the first step, the DMC should set out its objectives and vision for transformational reform. It will be important for the DMC to understand its endpoint ("to-be" state), or how far along the transformation road the tax administration would like to go.

Once the DMC has an idea of its endpoint, it needs to identify the baseline. The baseline is the present state of the tax administration's business processes and procedures, capacity, use of technology or technological readiness, and human resources. This step must consider taxpayer readiness and experience with digitized processes. A systematic diagnostic of the baseline is essential to developing a successful roadmap.

Figure 3: Steps Toward a Digital Transformation Roadmap

Vision and Goals	Assessment and Gap Analysis	Resources and Resource Arrangement	Cost and Benefit Analysis	Digital Roadmap
▸ Plan the vision based on the business vision of the tax authority. ▸ Reference to the experience of other peer tax authorities' digitalization journey. ▸ Establish short-term mid-term and long-term goals.	▸ Analyze the current state of tax filing process and identify pain points. ▸ Assessment of current tax compliance circumstances and potential tax gap analysis. ▸ Analysis of current processes and identify workflows will benefit from digitalization. ▸ Assessment of current IT environment, policies, legislation, infrastructure, application, information systems and development needs	▸ Evaluate current organizational structure and team members. ▸ Mapping of existing technology manpower. ▸ Assess the status of science and technology training.	▸ Stakeholder mapping. ▸ Current staff cost. ▸ Current infrastructure cost estimates. ▸ Estimate the time required and the cost-effectiveness that can be saved. ▸ Estimated digital budget—personnel, hardware and software. ▸ Prepare business case.	▸ Identify the interdependence of various factors. ▸ Define key milestones. ▸ Stakeholder management-insiders and taxpayers. ▸ Develop a timetable and roadmap: pilots and phasing.

IT = information technology.
Source: C. Sanger. 2020. Tax Authority Approaches to Digital Tax Administration. Ernst & Young Global Presentation. 30 October.

Next, a gap analysis is undertaken of the baseline and endpoint states. This assesses what is missing to move the DMC from baseline to endpoint state.

Using the findings from the gap analysis, the DMC can then decide the extent and speed of the transformation reform it seeks to undertake, bearing in mind the gap between the vision set out in the first step and what is possible considering resources and time required to get to the endpoint. It is also important to consider the principal stakeholders involved in the transformational reform, and their interactions, roles, responsibilities, and capacities.

The final step is the development of a digital transformation roadmap, which is a concrete, step-by-step plan to move from baseline to endpoint state. The roadmap consists of four phases: (i) mapping out the endpoint state; (ii) designing a reform that encompasses all necessary workstreams to get to the endpoint state; (iii) implementing the reform; and (iv) deploying the reform and testing it (Figure 4).

Based on the needs assessment, specific policy and administrative recommendations will be developed following best international practices. A roadmap—offering an approach to planning and monitoring a digital tax administration transformation journey—will also be prepared. The roadmap will set out a checklist and planning guide for each step of transformation and define milestones for progress.

This project is aligned with the ADB Strategy 2030 operational priority 6 (ADB 2018, ADB 2019), the ADB Pacific Approach objective 1 (ADB 2021), and the Strategic Priorities under the PITAA Strategic Plan 2022 to 2024.[4] This project also aligns with Nauru and Niue government efforts to leverage the potential of digital information systems to improve compliance and to enable tax administrations to be more effective and efficient.

Since the digital transformation of tax administration is a key component of a country's larger DRM agenda, ADB and the APTH aim to expand this project to include more DMCs in the future.

Figure 4: Summary of a Digital Transformation Roadmap

Source: ADB. 2022. Launching a Digital Tax Administration Transformation: What You Need to Know. Manila.

A NEW PROJECT IN THE PACIFIC

In September 2023, ADB—supported by the Domestic Resource Mobilization Trust Fund and in partnership with the Pacific Islands Tax Administrators Association (PITAA) and the IMF Pacific Financial Technical Assistance Centre—launched a pilot project to support the design of a country-specific roadmap for the digital transformation of the tax administrations of Nauru and Niue.

The development partners will work with Nauru and Niue tax officials to get a clear understanding of the tax administration's transformation strategies and vision. A needs assessment will be performed to determine the gaps in people, products, processes, and technology between the baseline situation and the endpoint.

Lead authors: Kaelen Onusko, public management specialist (taxation), Sectors Group-Public Sector Management and Governance, Asian Development Bank (ADB); and Go Nagata, public management specialist (taxation), Sectors Group-Public Sector Management and Governance, ADB.

Endnotes

[1] World Bank. World Development Indicators (accessed 4 October 2023).

[2] A tax revenue-to-ratio of 15% is now widely regarded as the minimum required for sustainable development.

[3] The term "ICT expenditure" comprises all expenses covering hardware infrastructure, digital communication infrastructure, computers, software, other ICT areas, and staff working in these areas.

[4] PITAA's Strategic Priorities are to drive domestic revenue mobilization for Pacific economies and support good practice revenue administration.

References

Asian Development Bank (ADB). 2018. *Strategy 2030: Achieving a Prosperous, Inclusive, Resilient, and Sustainable Asia and the Pacific.* Manila.

ADB. 2019. *Strategy 2030 Operational Plan for Priority 6: Strengthening Governance and Institutional Capacity, 2019–2024.* Manila.

ADB. 2020a. *A Comparative Analysis of Tax Administration in Asia and the Pacific: 2020 Edition.* Manila.

ADB. 2020b. ADB to Establish Regional Hub to Help Economies Improve Domestic Resource Mobilization and Tax Cooperation. *News Release.* 17 September.

ADB. 2021. *Pacific Approach, 2021–2025.* Manila.

ADB. 2022. *Launching a Digital Tax Administration Transformation: What You Need to Know.* Manila.

ADB. 2023. *Asian Development Outlook September 2023* Manila.

ADB. Forthcoming. A Comparative Analysis of Tax Administration in Asia and the Pacific: Seventh Edition. Manila.

ADB Institute. 2022. *Taxation of the Digital Economy: New Models in Asia and the Pacific.*

M. Sy et al. 2022. Funding the Future: Tax Revenue Mobilization in the Pacific Island Countries. *Departmental Paper No. 2022/015.* Washington, DC: IMF.

Organisation for Economic Co-operation and Development (OECD). 2023. *Revenue Statistics in Asia and the Pacific 2023: Strengthening Property Taxation in Asia.*

Pacific Financial Technical Assistance Centre. 2023. *Annual Report 2023.* Suva.

United Nations, Economic and Social Commission for Asia and the Pacific (ESCAP). 2022. *The Digitalization of Tax Administrations in Asia and the Pacific: A Manual for Practitioners.* Bangkok: ESCAP.

Importance of Tourism: Case of Pacific Island Economies

Many Pacific island economies (PIEs) have a high dependence on the tourism sector, which is a major source of employment and economic growth of the domestic economy. Tourism development has the potential to support sustainable and resilient growth, and—through its direct and indirect linkage with other sectors—provides additional sources of domestic revenue collection to governments. Tourism can be one of the enablers providing countries with the financing needed to achieve the Sustainable Development Goals and ultimately inclusive and broad-based growth. However, tapping into the potential of domestic resource mobilization through tourism development also requires improving the interlinkages between tourism and local economies. This policy brief highlights important findings from an upcoming Asian Development Bank (ADB) report *Tourism as Services Export: Current State, Vulnerabilities, Building Resilience.*

Tourism can make an important contribution to PIE export receipts and the domestic economy through its forward and backward linkages. This is particularly important in relaxing the constraints on countries' balance of payments and providing more stable sources of foreign exchange reserves. International tourist consumption of services—such as hotels and restaurants, travel agencies, tourist guide services, and others—becomes part of export earnings for the tourist recipient country. For most PIEs, tourism exports account for a significant proportion of their services exports and gross domestic product (GDP), reflecting the sector's importance in domestic and external sectors. While this offers opportunities in tourism, it also brings challenges from external shocks, particularly when most of these countries are not diversified in their economic activities. In some PIEs such as Palau—where tourism is the predominant driver of economic activity—tourism also has important fiscal implications (see page 12). This brief recommends that PIEs not only enhance international tourist inflow—and hence services exports—but also diversify their economic activities to make them resilient to external shocks.

Tourism exports constitute a major share of PIE services exports. In 2019, the share was more than 50% in many PIEs compared to an average of about 31% for the Asia and Pacific region. The share was as high as 89% for Tuvalu, followed by Vanuatu (85%) and Fiji (84%) in 2019 (Figure 5). Many PIEs had a more than 50% share of tourism exports relative to total exports of goods and services in 2019. For the top three PIEs, the shares were 86.0% (Tuvalu), 73.0% (Vanuatu), and 62.0% (Samoa) compared with an average of 5.8% for the Asia and Pacific region. The high dependence on tourism indicates limited economic diversification in these countries. This makes PIEs vulnerable to external shocks such as those observed during the coronavirus disease (COVID-19) pandemic.

Tourism exports in PIEs constitute a very low share of overall exports in Asia and the Pacific. In 2019, this group of countries generated $2.3 billion in tourism exports, which is only about 0.5% of $486.0 billion for the Asia and Pacific region. The low share largely reflects the small size of the PIEs especially compared to the rest of the region. It also suggests a potential to increase tourism exports through appropriate policy interventions. Figure 6 shows tourism exports of individual PIE countries in 2019, with Fiji taking the lead, followed by Vanuatu, the Cook Islands, and Samoa.

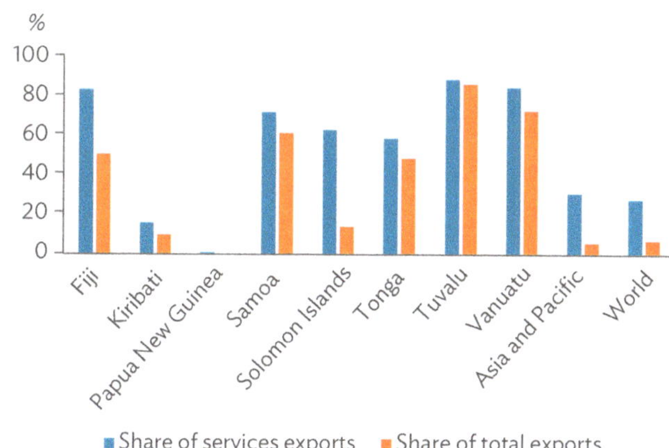

Figure 5: Tourism Exports for Pacific Island Economies and the Asia and Pacific Region, 2019

Source: Authors' estimates based on United Nations World Tourism Organization Dashboard. Global and Regional Tourism Performance (accessed May 2023).

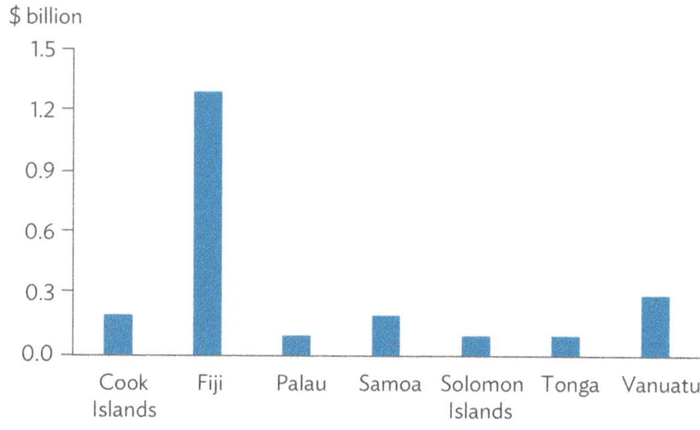

Figure 6: Pacific Tourism Exports, 2019

Note: Data not available for the Federated States of Micronesia, Nauru, and Niue. For Kiribati, the Marshall Islands, Papua New Guinea, and Tuvalu, tourism exports were less than $100 million and would have shown up as negligible in this figure.

Source: Authors' estimates based on United Nations World Tourism Organization Dashboard. Global and Regional Tourism Performance (accessed May 2023).

While the total tourism receipts by PIEs were small compared to the Asia and Pacific region, the gap was much narrower for per-arrival receipts. In 2019, PIEs earned $2 billion ($1,162 per arrival) and the Asia and Pacific earned $441 billion ($1,225 per arrival) in tourism receipts. The per-arrival receipts for the Pacific subregion were higher than the global average of $1,019 in 2019 (Figure 7). The tourism receipts per arrival in the Pacific indicate relatively high-paying visitors to the subregion, which could be attributed in part to the higher cost of tourism services. Among the PIEs, Fiji led in tourism receipts (Figure 8a), but the Cook Islands, Solomon Islands, and Vanuatu also had high per-arrival tourism receipts (Figure 8b).

Tourism exports constitute a significant share of PIE GDP, though there is variation among countries. The $2.3 billion in PIE tourism exports in 2019 constituted about 6.5% of the GDP of the subregion. This is high when compared to other subregions in Asia and the Pacific, where Southeast Asia is 4.8%, South Asia is 1.1%, and East Asia is 0.8% (Figure 9). This implies that the Pacific subregion is relatively more dependent on tourism exports for their domestic economies.

Tourism exports as a percentage of GDP reflect significant variation within the region. More than 20% of GDP comes from tourism exports in Fiji, Palau, Samoa, and Vanuatu, highlighting limited economic diversification of these economies (Figure 10).

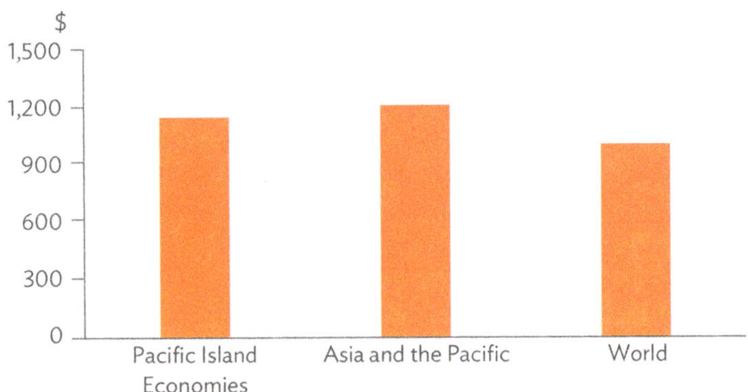

Figure 7: Per Arrival Tourism Receipts, 2019

Source: Authors' estimates based on United Nations World Tourism Organization Dashboard. Global and Regional Tourism Performance (accessed May 2023).

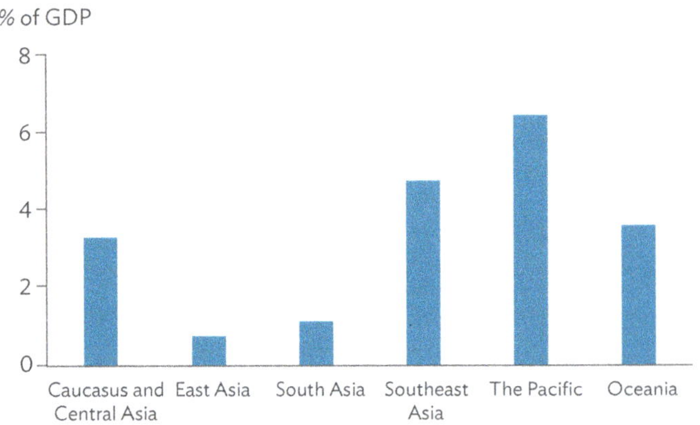

Figure 9: Tourism Exports in Asia and the Pacific, 2019

GDP = gross domestic product.

Note: Caucasus comprises Armenia, Azerbaijan, Georgia, Kazakhstan, Kyrgyz Republic, Tajikistan, Turkmenistan, and Uzbekistan. Oceania comprises Australia and New Zealand.

Source: Authors' estimates based on United Nations World Tourism Organization Dashboard. Global and Regional Tourism Performance (accessed May 2023).

Tourism exports have important implications for the domestic economy. International tourists create demand for goods and services locally, creating employment and raising foreign direct investment in upstream and downstream activities. Tourism exports, thereby, contribute to GDP, employment, and foreign exchange reserves.

Figure 8a and 8b: Pacific Tourism Receipts and Per Arrival Receipts, 2019

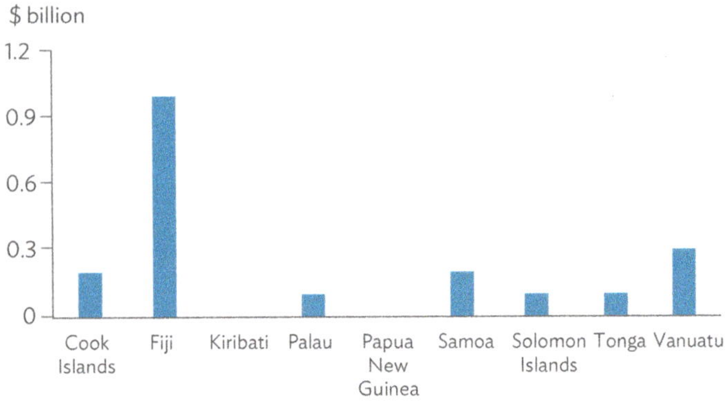

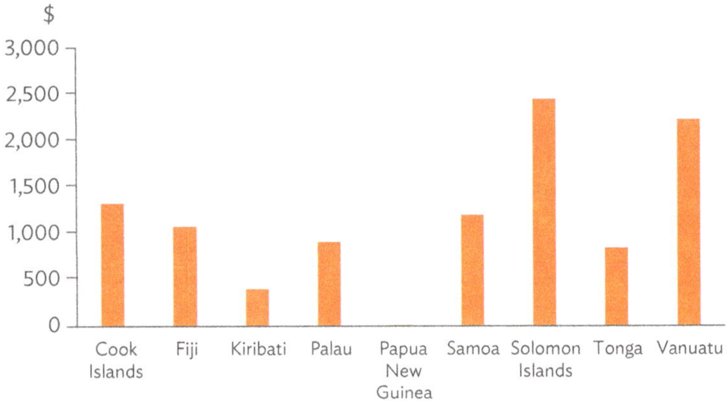

Source: Authors' estimates based on United Nations World Tourism Organization Dashboard. Global and Regional Tourism Performance (accessed May 2023).

It should be noted that tourism exports—as a services export entry—can help improve a country's balance of payments position contributing to overall macroeconomic stability. As an important source of foreign exchange reserves—especially for tourism-dependent economies—tourism exports can help offset a trade deficit through enhanced services export earnings and reduce current account deficits.[1]

As the tourism sector offers a multidimensional product, it is likely to lead to changes in the pattern of demand and generate new economic activities. This can potentially provide PIEs with new sources of domestic revenue. For example, improving infrastructure, hotel facilities, and providing better transportation facilities can promote domestic industries and provide a potential source of collecting tax revenues. Viewed in this context, a vibrant tourism sector not only provides foreign exchange but also additional sources of domestic revenue that contribute to fiscal space.

Among PIEs, tourism exports largely offset merchandise trade deficits and act as a source of foreign exchange earnings. Except for Papua New Guinea, almost all PIEs have a merchandise trade deficit (Table 3). However, a number of them run a current account surplus, implying that tourism exports are helping these countries to mitigate the deficits in their merchandise trade accounts. In countries like the Cook Islands, Fiji, Solomon Islands, and Vanuatu, tourism exports as a percent of the trade balance is more than 100%, implying that tourism exports are not only offsetting the trade deficit but are also generating a surplus in the current account of the balance of payments. Thus, tourism exports are an important source of foreign exchange reserves for economies in this region.

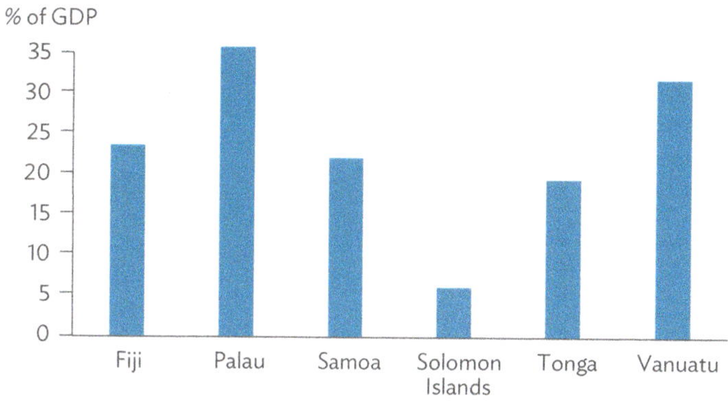

Figure 10: Pacific Tourism Exports, 2019

GDP = gross domestic product.

Note: Data not available for the Federated States of Micronesia, Nauru, and Niue. Values for Kiribati, the Marshall Islands, Papua New Guinea, and Tuvalu would have appeared as negligible in this figure.

Source: Authors' estimates based on United Nations World Tourism Organization Dashboard. Global and Regional Tourism Performance (accessed May 2023).

On the whole, the Pacific subregion comprising small-sized economies is significantly dependent on tourism for its domestic and external sectors. This puts these economies at risk, particularly to external shocks affecting tourism inflows.

The Pacific was one of the worst-affected subregions during the COVID-19 pandemic. Tourism exports for this region became almost zero in 2021. As a percentage of services exports, tourism

Table 3: Pacific Tourism Exports and External Sector Indicators, 2019

	Current Account Balance (% of GDP)	Trade Balance ($ billion)	Tourism Exports ($ billion)	Tourism Exports (% of Trade Balance)
Cook Islands	33.2	(0.12)	0.2	165.5
Federated States of Micronesia	23.1	(0.13)	NA	NA
Fiji	(4.7)	(0.96)	1.3	135.7
Kiribati	48.5	(0.09)	0.0	0.0
Marshall Islands	(24.4)	(0.13)	0.0	0.0
Nauru	4.9	(0.05)	NA	NA
Niue	NA	NA	NA	NA
Palau	(31.1)	(0.14)	0.1	69.9
Papua New Guinea	22.1	7.47	0.0	0.0
Samoa	3.0	(0.30)	0.2	66.8
Solomon Islands	(9.8)	(0.04)	0.1	274.0
Tonga	(0.8)	(0.21)	0.1	48.6
Tuvalu	(16.9)	(0.04)	0.0	0.0
Vanuatu	12.8	(0.28)	0.3	108.7

( ) = negative, GDP = gross domestic product, NA = not applicable.

Source: Authors' estimates based on data from Asian Development Bank. Asian Development Outlook database, Current Account Balance in Asia and the Pacific (accessed May 2023) and United Nations World Tourism Organization Dashboard. Global and Regional Tourism Performance (accessed May 2023).

Table 4: Tourism Exports in Asia and the Pacific, Before and During COVID-19

Subregion	Tourism Exports ($ billion)		
	2019	2020	2021
Caucasus and Central Asia	12.7	2.5	4.3
East Asia	163.4	38.2	30.3
South Asia	41.4	16.8	13.6
Southeast Asia	155.2	33.1	11.0
The Pacific	2.3	0.3	0.0
Oceania	58.2	32.2	19.9

COVID-19 = coronavirus disease.

Note: Caucasus comprises Armenia, Azerbaijan, Georgia, Kazakhstan, Kyrgyz Republic, Tajikistan, Turkmenistan, and Uzbekistan. Oceania comprises Australia and New Zealand.

Source: Authors' estimates based on United Nations World Tourism Organization Dashboard. Global and Regional Tourism Performance (accessed May 2023).

exports declined by about 87% in 2020 and by 100% in 2021 compared to the 2019 level. The fall in exports due to the external shock to tourism services exceeded the decline in overall services exports. The decrease in tourism exports in the Pacific subregion was the largest among all the subregions of Asia and the Pacific (Table 4, Figure 11). In Fiji, Samoa, Solomon Islands, Tuvalu, and Vanuatu, tourism exports as a percentage of services exports declined sharply in 2020 and 2021 compared to 2019 (pre-COVID-19).

Tourism exports contribution to GDP became negligible in 2021 as receipts fell to almost zero after the PIEs completely closed their borders during the pandemic. Countries like Fiji, Palau, Samoa, Tonga, and Vanuatu suffered severe setbacks compared to the sector's high contribution in 2019.

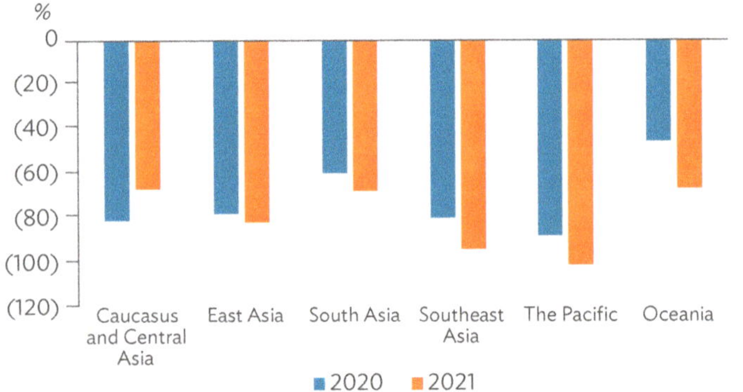

Figure 11: Percentage Decline in Tourism Exports compared to 2019, Asia and the Pacific Subregions

( ) = negative.

Note: Caucasus comprises Armenia, Azerbaijan, Georgia, Kazakhstan, Kyrgyz Republic, Tajikistan, Turkmenistan, and Uzbekistan. Oceania comprises Australia and New Zealand.

Source: Authors' estimates based on United Nations World Tourism Organization Dashboard. Global and Regional Tourism Performance (accessed May 2023).

Analysis shows that there is a significantly high correlation between tourism exports as the percentage of services exports (pre-COVID-19) and the percentage decline in tourism exports during the pandemic (Figure 12) for the Pacific subregion. Although this may be an indication of the small size and island economy characteristics of PIEs, it should be noted that the PIEs were among the last to open their borders because of healthcare systems that were relatively ill-equipped to tackle the pandemic. While closing borders contained the spread of the virus, it resulted in almost zero international tourist arrivals to these countries, severely affecting employment, income, and other macroeconomic parameters. This emphasizes the need for alternative policy options to sustain tourism flow while ensuring the health and safety of the local population.

Comparing the PIEs with the Maldives—another small island economy in South Asia—it was observed that the Maldives experienced modest growth in tourism exports during the pandemic years when other similar small island economies in the Pacific were contracting. The better tourism performance could be attributed to aggressive policies to attract international tourists as early as when lockdown restrictions began easing in 2020. This approach helped improve the confidence of international tourists. The Maldives worked on re-branding and marketing itself to promote a better image during the pandemic. It came up with a marketing campaign with the tagline "Isolation never looked this good" in 2020 to emphasize Maldives as a niche destination (Blackman 2022). This highlights the role of suitable policy interventions in managing tourism resilience going forward.

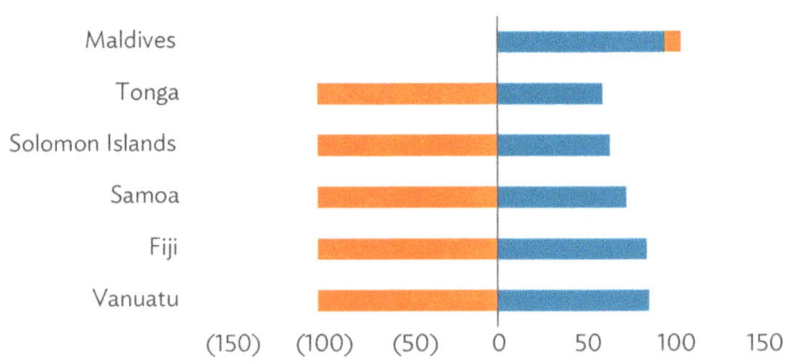

Figure 12: Tourism Exports as Percentage of Services Exports (pre-COVID) and Percentage Decline in Tourism Exports during the Pandemic

( ) = negative, COVID-19 = coronavirus disease.

Source: Authors' estimates.

Given the high dependence of the Pacific subregion on international tourist inflows and tourism exports, policy planning and implementation at the country, regional, and global levels are crucial to building resilience.

- Improved connectivity is a key enabler for enhancing international tourism. For PIEs, cross-border air connectivity is crucial. Besides augmenting capacity for hard infrastructure, regional and bilateral open skies policies can facilitate travel by raising the number of airlines flying between signatory countries, the number of destinations covered, the number of seats. Governments in the Pacific may learn ways to enhance regulatory cooperation over air connectivity from the experience of other Asia and Pacific subregions.

- Many Pacific economies depend heavily on tourists from specific countries. For example, most international tourists visiting Fiji are from Australia, New Zealand, and the US. This dependence makes tourism exports in Fiji vulnerable to external shocks affecting the source countries. Proactive government intervention is needed to diversify source countries for international tourists to minimize damage from specific external shocks. Bilateral cooperation arrangements and establishing travel bubbles or tourism corridors can be useful policies in this respect.

- PIE governments should consider cooperation agreements within and outside the region for visa exemption and visa-on-arrival facilities if providing these facilities is not universally feasible. Cooperation agreements with transit countries should be useful for economies in the region as many PIEs have limited direct connectivity with other parts of the world, which necessitates international tourists transiting through other countries to reach their final destinations.

- PIEs are feared to have limited carrying capacity. This necessitates governments pooling their tourism resources and marketing themselves as an integrated tourist destination to facilitate travelers visiting multiple tourist destinations or islands. In 2020, Australia started the Pacific Flights Program that subsidizes air services connecting Brisbane with the Central and North Pacific. Greater intra-regional connectivity is essential for positioning the Pacific as an integrated tourist destination. While this will help to realize economies of scale, it will also distribute international tourists more uniformly across PIEs, allaying concerns over limited individual carrying capacities.

- Policies should also focus on the diversification of economic activities, particularly with the PIEs having tourism exports as more than 100% of their trade balance. Since the tourism sector has close interlinkages with other sectors, tourism can be used as a positive way to develop other PIE industries such as garments or souvenir-related manufacturing. These products also hold good export potential if they can be customized to the tastes and preferences of international tourists.

- Countries may consider specialized policies focusing on tourism exports as most of them lack dedicated policies to promote tourism as an export sector. In other words, existing policies related to tourism focus on the tourism sector in general— including domestic tourism—and may lack discussion as to its contribution to services exports. Such policies may have export-linked subsidies and incentives for this sector.

- The PIEs should adopt and implement unilateral policies that have positive effects on tourism both from the demand and supply sides. For instance, unilateral policies—such as foreign direct investment policies and investment incentives—can help to augment the supply of tourism services offerings, whereas easier tourist visa policies—such as visa free access and visa on arrival— contribute to increasing the demand for tourism services.

- Intraregional cooperation for tourism services through the involvement of other stakeholders—such as industry associations—should also be explored. Such cooperation could involve activities such as capacity-building, resource sharing, technology upgrading, and knowledge exchange.

- As negotiations on services have stalled at the multilateral level (i.e., the World Trade Organization), multilateral policies may not play an important role in tourism development in this subregion as of 2023. However, the PIEs may consider identifying regulatory barriers in other countries that affect their international tourism inflows and take these up for discussion on services trade issues at the World Trade Organization.

Lead authors: Sanchita Basu Das, economist, Economic Research and Development Impact Department, ADB; and Pralok Gupta, associate professor (services and investment), Centre for WTO Studies, Indian Institute of Foreign Trade.

Endnote

[1] The current account in the balance of payments monitors the transaction of funds for the import and export of goods and services between a country and the rest of the world. A current account deficit (surplus) occurs when the country's expenditure on imports is greater (less) than its receipts from exports of goods and services. It is generally measured as a percentage of GDP. The trade balance is a component of the current account and is measured as the difference between merchandise (goods) exports and merchandise imports. A trade surplus (deficit) occurs when receipts from merchandise exports are greater (less) than payments for merchandise imports.

References

Asian Development Bank (ADB). 2023. Tourism as Services Export: Current State, Vulnerabilities, Building Resilience. Manila. (Forthcoming).

ADB. Asian Development Outlook database, Current Account Balance in Asia and the Pacific. (accessed May 2023).

V. M. Blackman. 2022. The Changing Face of Tourism and Work: How Maldives Is Successfully Adapting to the Pandemic. *World Bank Blog*. 26 January.

United Nations World Tourism Organization Dashboard. Global and Regional Tourism Performance (accessed May 2023).

Nonfuel Merchandise Exports from Australia
(A$; y-o-y % change, 3-month m.a.)

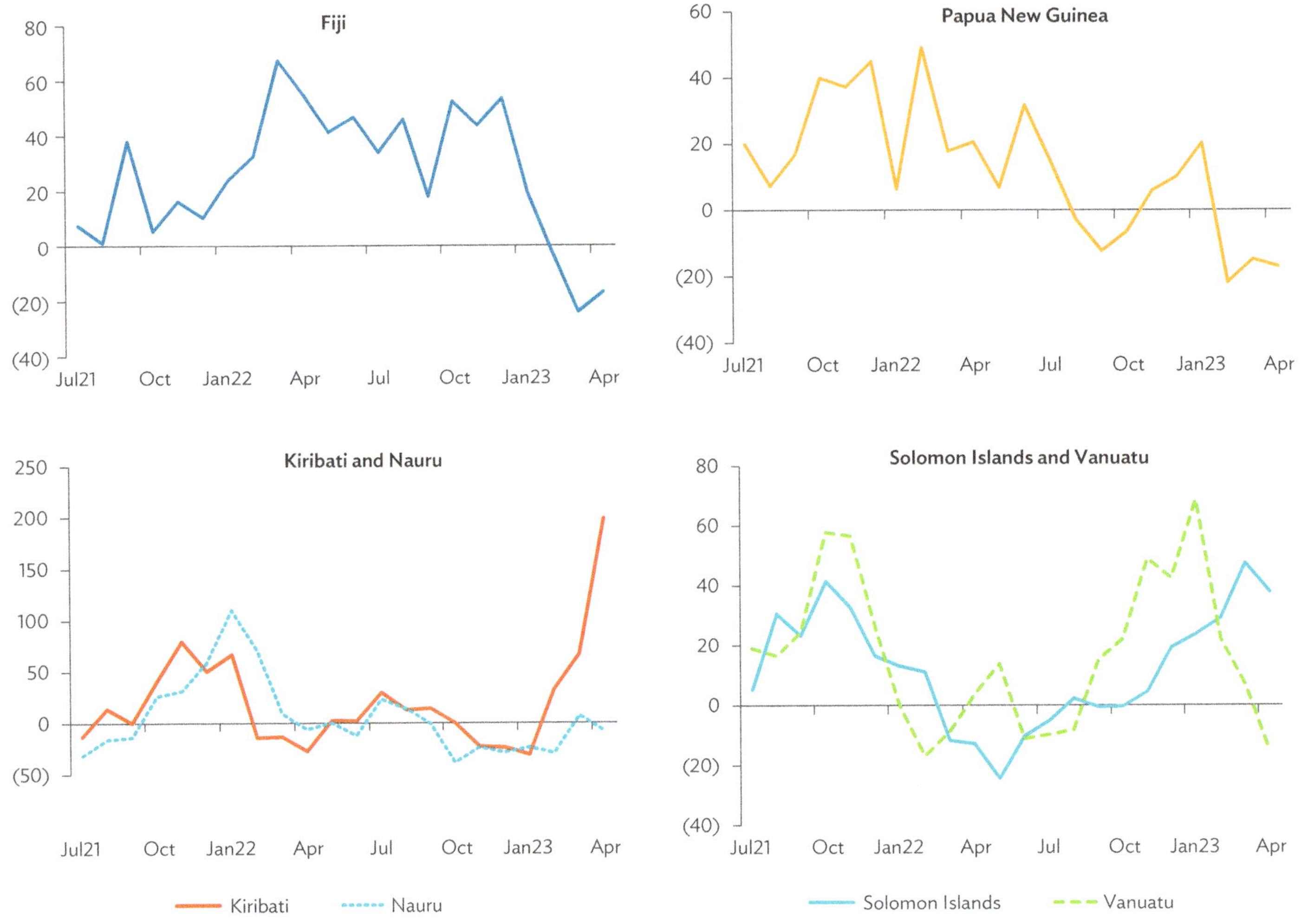

Fiji
Papua New Guinea
Kiribati and Nauru
Solomon Islands and Vanuatu
Jul21
Oct
Jan22
Apr
Jul
Oct
Jan23
Apr
Kiribati
Nauru
Solomon Islands
Vanuatu

( ) = negative, A$ = Australian dollar, m.a. = moving average, y-o-y = year-on-year.
Source: Australian Bureau of Statistics.

Nonfuel Merchandise Exports from New Zealand and the United States
(y-o-y % change, 3-month m.a.)

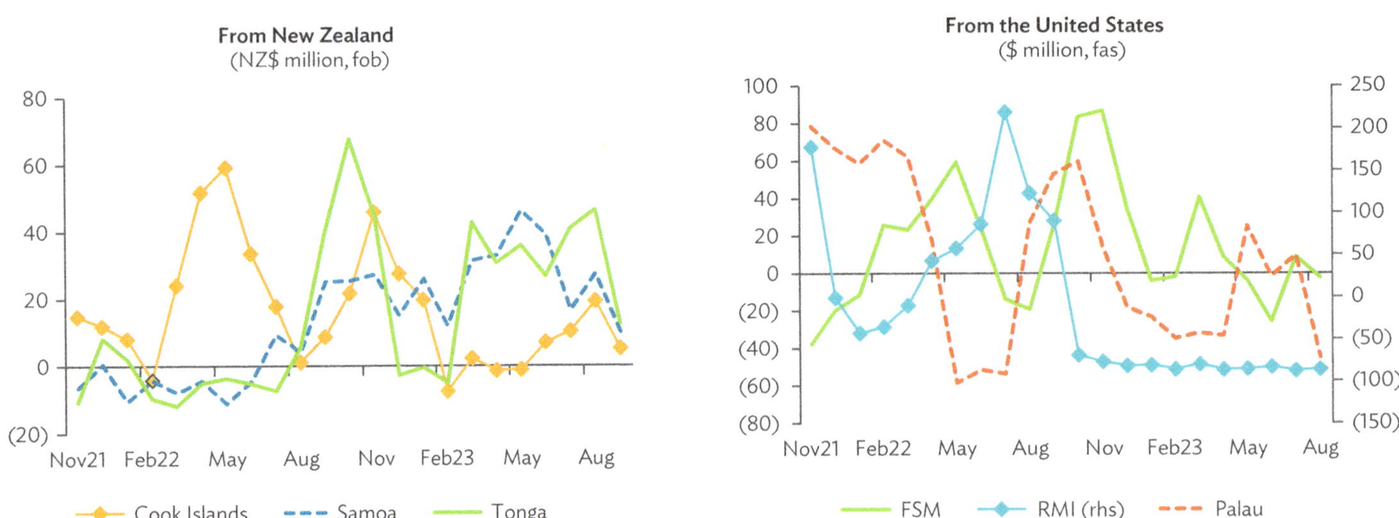

From New Zealand
(NZ$ million, fob)
From the United States
($ million, fas)
Nov21
Feb22
May
Aug
Nov
Feb23
May
Aug
Cook Islands
Samoa
Tonga
FSM
RMI (rhs)
Palau

( ) = negative, fas = free alongside, fob = free on board, FSM = Federated States of Micronesia, m.a. = moving average, NZ$ = New Zealand dollar, rhs = right-hand scale, RMI = Republic of the Marshall Islands, y-o-y = year on year.
Sources: Statistics New Zealand and United States Census Bureau.

Diesel Exports from Singapore
(y-o-y % change, 3-month m.a.)

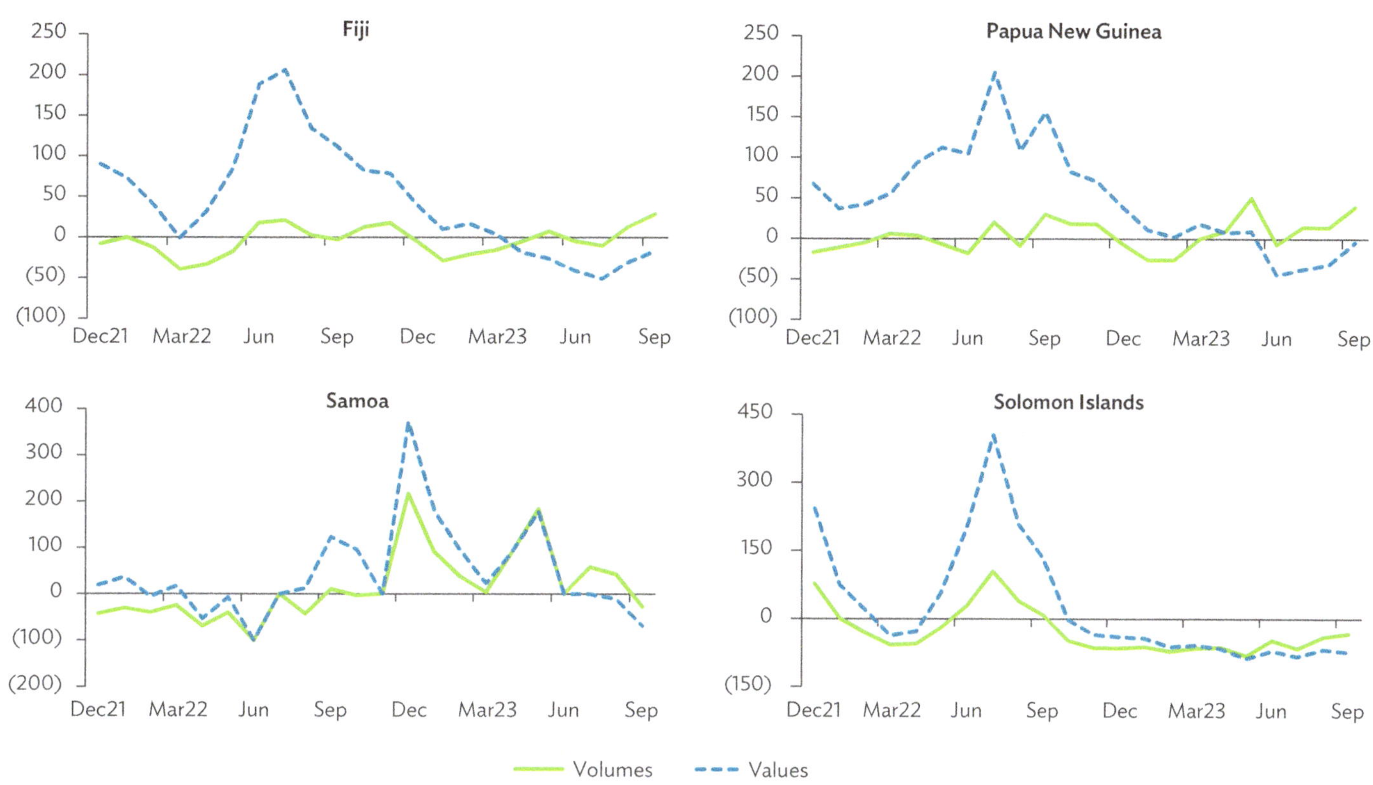

( ) = negative, m.a. = moving average, y-o-y = year on year.

Source: International Enterprise Singapore.

Gasoline Exports from Singapore
(y-o-y % change, 3-month m.a.)

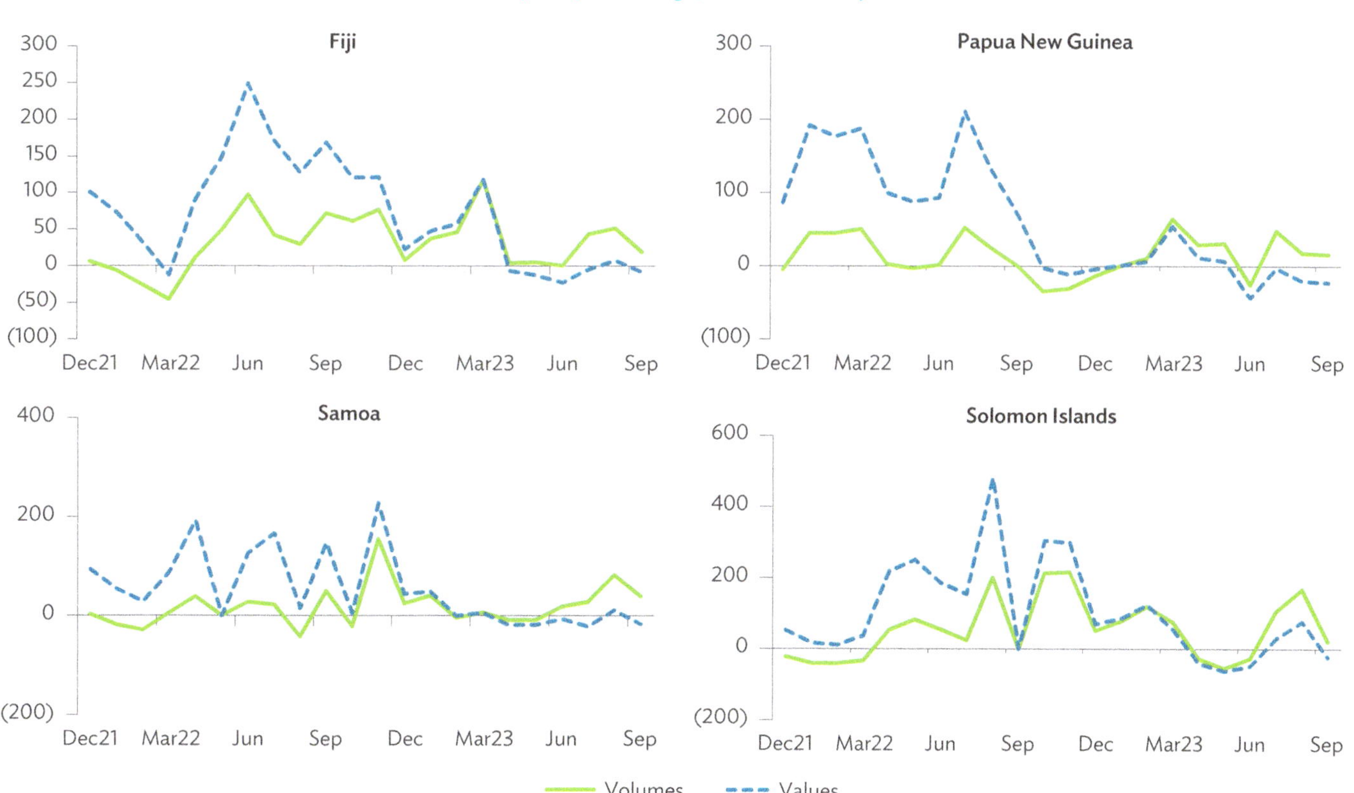

( ) = negative, m.a. = moving average, y-o-y = year on year.

Source: International Enterprise Singapore.

Departures from Australia to the Pacific
(monthly)

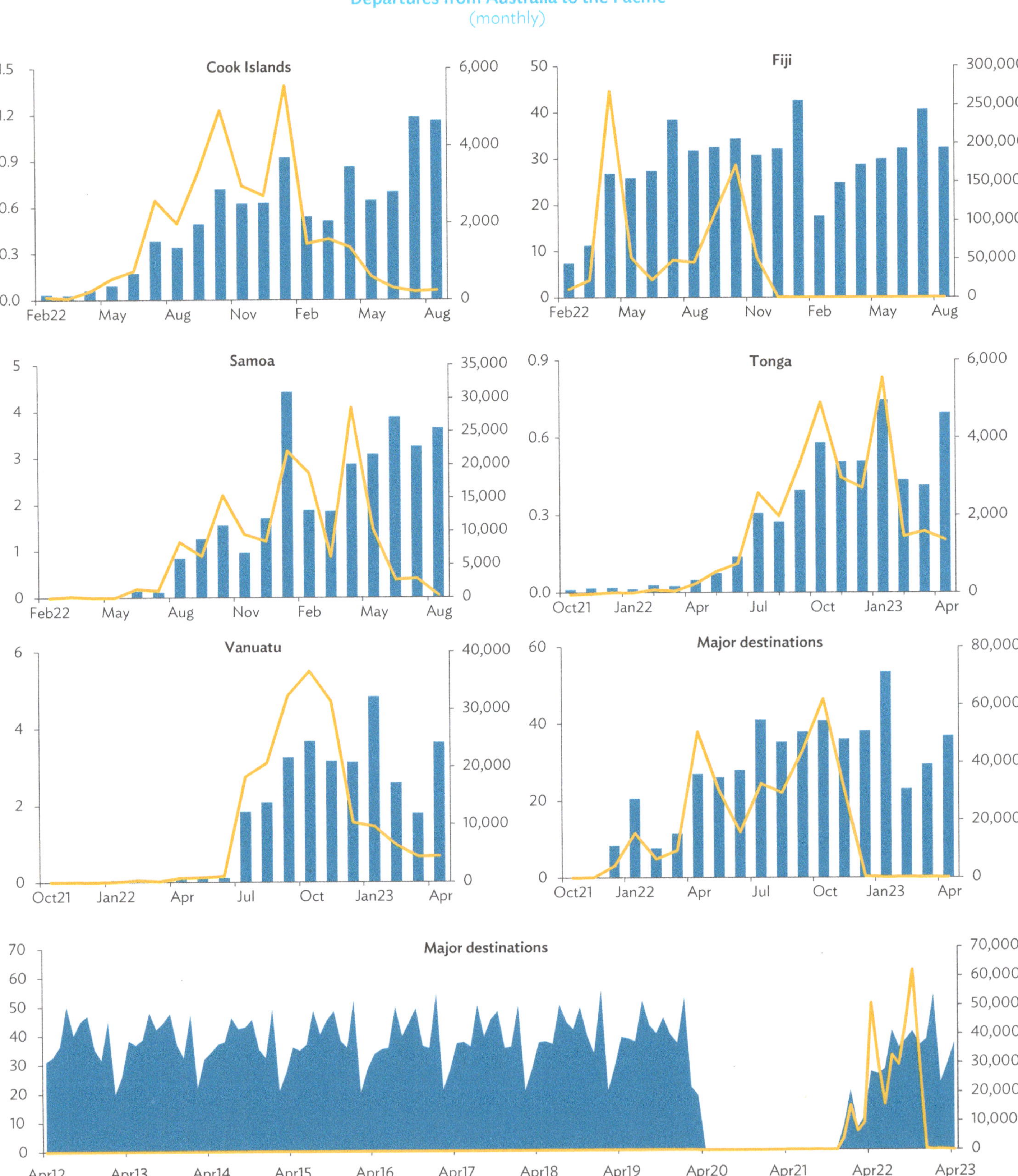

( ) = negative, rhs = right-hand scale, y-o-y = year on year.
Source: Australian Bureau of Statistics.

Departures from New Zealand to the Pacific
(monthly)

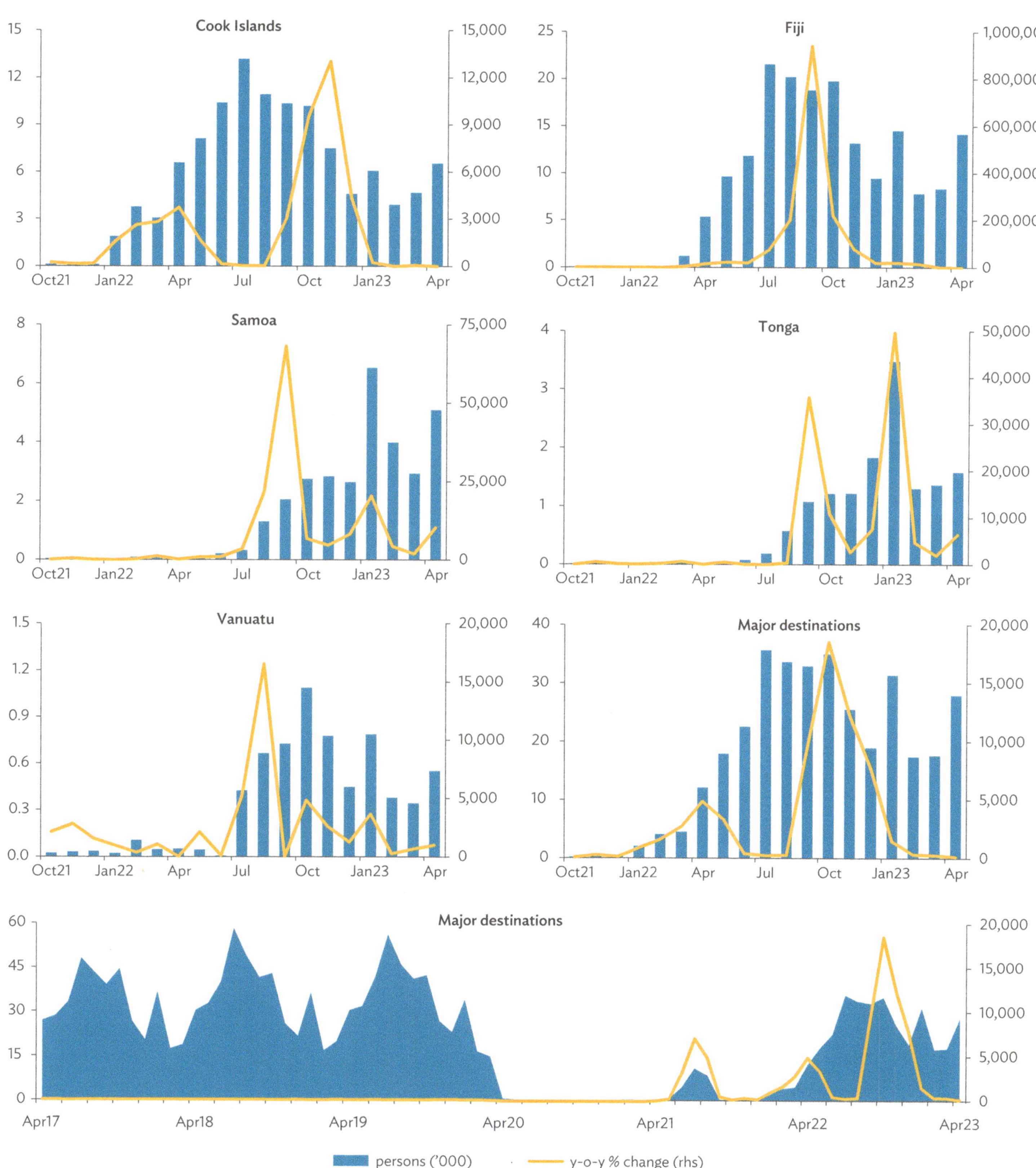

( ) = negative, rhs = right-hand scale, y-o-y = year-on-year.
Source: Statistics New Zealand.